Soul Fire

Soul Fire

Choose to Live

By Sarah Kelly

A book about human resilience, love, and overcoming. It's about believing in yourself and digging deep into your heart to find the strength to heal.

Happy Books Ink, LLC
Virginia Beach

For privacy reasons, some names, locations, and dates may have been changed.

SOUL FIRE

Copyright © 2024 by Sarah Kelly
All rights reserved.

No part of this publication may be reproduced, distributed, or transmitted in any form or by any means, including photocopying, recording, or other electronic or mechanical methods, without the prior written permission of the publisher, except as permitted by U.S. copyright law. For permission requests, contact Happy Books Ink, LLC.

Published by Happy Books Ink, LLC
1385 Fordham Dr. Suite 105 - Box 242
Virginia Beach, VA 23464

happy.books.ink@gmail.com

ISBN 978-1-966055-00-6 (hardcover)

Book Cover Art by Dyanne Joyner

First edition, November 2024
Second printing, August 2025

Table of Contents

0.	Introduction	i
1.	Surrender to Live	1
2.	Stress is Not Worth Your Life	15
3.	The Door I Wasn't Willing to Walk Through	25
4.	Hiding	47
5.	Anxiety: The Not-So-Shiny Bits	57
6.	Fear Lies To You	77
7.	Forgiveness	101
8.	Mom's Journey	115
9.	I Gotta Pee	127
10.	Celebrate Every Step	139
11.	"Post" Illness: Living Again	149
12.	Grief Isn't a Competition	161
13.	Am I an Orphan or an Elder?	169
14.	I Danced Today: Staying Alive	177
15.	Overcoming	187
16.	Choose to Live	195
17.	Aneurysm Alley	205
18.	Just in Time	219
19.	Signs and Miracles	225
20.	Angels	237
21.	WWDD: What would Dad Do?	245
22.	The Painted Desert Life	255
23.	Grace and Kindness	263
24.	Acknowledgements	271

Key Points of Healing

The key points of healing are the threads that hold the book together.

The Flame

At the beginning of each chapter, you will find something I had to buy into in order to heal. Each chapter and topic held a belief I had to alter in order to move forward.

The Fuel

The fuel was what I gave myself through my healing, the "so what", if you will. When I healed from the issue, I received the gift of that particular fuel. Inevitably, the fuel sustained me and helped me move through the next piece of healing.

Together, they help to make up my Soul Fire.

Warning: The contents of this book may be triggering to some readers. Content includes grief, death of a parent, health struggles, stroke recovery, suicide, and trauma. Names and specific details have been changed in some cases to protect the identities of individuals living or deceased.

This book is based solely on my life and my experiences and is not in any way linked to other organizations or religions. I use the term Universe throughout the book deliberately. It's meant to be respectful. I value your individual spirituality, religion, or lack thereof. The message and path to healing is meant to be louder than any specific faith. Feel free to insert whatever word you wish instead of Universe if it bothers you. The beliefs and conclusions I have come to are my own.

For everyone who's ever lost someone to suicide, violence, or tragedy, I'm sorry. There are no words to express what you've gone through and no magic fix. Some people are taken from us without reason. The soul ripping pain created with that horrible act of violence is unimaginably deep and unexplainable. Please know, if you or someone you know has gone through something like that, my heart aches for you.

My family shaped me in so many ways. My mom taught me how to love. Dad taught me how a woman should be treated. He taught me about healthy boundaries. Women in my life have taught me about loving myself and what mark I wanted to make in this life. These people are the village that helped raise me so I could share the lessons.

Life throws us curve balls. I've had several one after another. I started a business from the fear of my husband dying from repeated strokes. Shocker, it

Introduction

didn't work out the way I had planned. My mother moved closer to us at the end of her life. The week of the Pandemic shutdown, she was diagnosed with metastatic stage four cancer. She died within three months. I got COVID just after she died. I could have given up. I could have given in to the deep fear and sorrow completely.

I began writing when I was in the throes of COVID, unable to breathe freely. I was choking on my own fluid, had searing pain, and could not rest. I did not know if I would see another daybreak. The one clear thought I had was that I had something to say before it was too late. Hours later, the words kept coming as the sun traversed the horizon at 6:30 in the morning. What started as a necessity has revealed itself as my life's work. Healing. I threw my hands up and said yes to the Universe. I began sharing my story. May it give you hope and love and permission to live.

Surrender to Live

Accepting that my dad was dying required me to surrender to the truth. I didn't have to be happy he was dying. It happened independent of my feelings on the matter.

Surrender often comes when I least expect it and least want it. Surrendering, in general is not my preferred method. Dad taught me how to surrender to live. It was a hard-earned lesson.

My heart was pounding out of my chest. Breathing took all the effort I had. I could feel pressure in both carotid arteries on the sides of my neck and blood coursing in my aorta. As a former EMT and pre-med student, I knew enough to know that was not normal. Unable to focus on the game and almost to the point of hyperventilating, I excused myself from our family board game and went into an empty room. I sat down on the hardwood floor and prayed. I prayed to slow my pulse; I prayed to breathe easier; and I prayed for the impossible, that my father would live. In those moments, praying for my father's life, I knew it was I who had to "surrender to live" - just as I'd told Dad prior to his aneurysm surgery ten days before.

Sitting on the floor, feeling naked and raw, I became aware that every defense mechanism I'd ever built had been stripped away. A shroud of five years of constant stress over the health of several beloved family members fell into a raging river of emotions, revealing the tightly woven web of my life.

Every single decision I'd made since I was a teenager was one to either hide or survive. But until that moment, I hadn't allowed myself to accept how much of the time I spent hiding. Survivors are strong and fearless, right? They must never show weakness, or they'll be taken advantage of. Or at least that's what my inner survivor had always told me.

In the days preceding my dad's aneurysm surgery, I had an ominous feeling. Dad lived with us for five years prior to his death. He had a good strong name, Paul. I always loved the name because it was his. He, being a junior, never cared much for it. Paul had already survived two strokes. He was also a writer who self-published three books, including one about stroke recovery. He was my caring, doting, loving father. He was my rock.

My heart was breaking as I helped him gather his things and make his way to the car. My gut clenched as he descended the stairs. I gave him every ounce of my patience and love, especially that day. His gait was shaky, tentative, and unsure. His back was hunched over, as it never used to be in his younger years. His oversized jeans looked so big on him. The white tennis shoes squeaked across the hardwood floor. He scuffed them getting out of the wheelchair and grabbing onto the railing in the garage. The three stairs seemed like much more as time slowed. He had to carefully place his body in order to stay safe as he navigated the world. Relief crossed his face as he and his sky-blue sweater flopped into the front seat of the four-door sedan. The zipper banged on the outside of the car as he fell back. I held my breath praying he didn't hit his head or injure himself anywhere. I turned my face away to hide the worry and sadness I felt.

Slowly, I walked around the car as if on death march, looking at the smooth gray concrete floor of the garage. Carefully and deliberately, I sat in the driver's seat feeling immense guilt and sadness. I did not take my own mobility for granted. I wanted so badly to fix this for him.

Every car trip no matter the duration required quality music choices. The six CD changer had been state of the art when we bought the car. I remembered Dad's station wagon, filled with clear plastic 1980's cassette tapes with their white words printed on the outside. I could visualize the thin brown tape and the white plastic wheels it wound around as I glanced at the dash to pick a CD. We weren't in his car today.

What would we listen to for this ride? Instinctively, I knew it would be his last ride in the car. The choice, weighing heavy, had to be Garth Brooks. As "The Dance" and "The River" played from one of his many albums, Paul listened. His eyes closed as he listened to the beginning beats and melody. He smiled and looked out at the trees and the sky from his seat.

Weeks ago, I'd voiced my concerns about his surgery and let it be. It was his choice, not mine. The new doctor didn't think his declining physical status bore any weight on his aorta replacement surgery.

"If you make it out of surgery, Dad, you'll have a lot of rehab to do."

"What do you mean If?" Dad said with some alarm.

"I just mean it's a huge surgery and I'm trying to see where you're at with it. Losing your core strength from a long vertical incision will take something from you temporarily. How do you feel?"

"I've done it before, after the strokes. I'm no stranger to working hard."

I took a deep breath in, let go of the fear and lost myself in the music and the moments around me. We could talk to each other frankly about anything. This conversation hadn't been easy. It was important for me to understand where he was emotionally. He had given me the tough job of being his champion with medical decisions if he couldn't make them. I had to be clear on his wants in order to best serve him. Knowing didn't make it easier.

I told him how much I loved him as we got into the pre-operating room. Paul made amends with his ex-wife, my mother. Per usual, I was the go between. That day, it felt cathartic and foreboding as I texted Mom. I remembered how Dad had soothed my soul years before with a salve of his tough words. He told me I had to **surrender to win.** Those words helped me through a very tough birth and c-section for a beautiful baby boy.

The day I realized my father was dying was the same day I was told that my young husband would live through his own six strokes and brain aneurysm. Ten days into my father's so called "recovery", he was on a ventilator and unable to breathe on his own. His heartbeat was not regular without stabilizing drugs. Three times the breathing tube came out and three times he could not breathe. Dad was known as Paul to the rest of the world. To me, he was my rock, my protector, my musician, and my teacher. When he died, all the places I had hidden were laid bare. I knew at that moment, **I had to surrender to live**. It was my time to choose to live.

I am a survivor. By eleven years old, I was giving advice on what bills should be paid in order to keep the lights and the heat from being turned off. I'm a child of an alcoholic, a seeker of wisdom, and one who wants to get it right. As a teenager, my stepfather threatened to kill me multiple times. For the past five years, I've been on a journey of self-discovery and introspection. As I was losing my father, I saw the ramifications of denial for the first time ever. By not admitting I had been terrified as a teenager, I spent twenty-five years in hiding and alone. In those moments of grief and change, I agreed to say yes to things and not hide anymore.

There are triggers in our lives. Some of them remind us of old wounds. Some of them break open our protective shells and encourage us to let go of the past pain. My father's death was my trigger to evolve. That journey took me from hiding, to saying yes. I went from feeling utterly and completely alone in the world to someone who feels seen and known.

I often see the old things in the current scenarios. As my father was dying, it hit me. I saw all the ways I had hidden my light, dimmed myself, and made myself small in order to survive. I saw myself through my children's eyes. I realized I wanted to be someone they could be proud to have as their mom. I understood that I had to live in order to be that someone. I had to surrender to win.

Reality check: My father was dying. What now? Reality checks can be like being hit with a sledgehammer. You're coasting along 'fine' one day, and then stopped dead in your tracks with a wakeup call so big that all your survival mechanisms get ripped away from the old wound you hide from the world. Surviving was not enough anymore. The band aid was circling the drain. Just staying alive was no longer enough. I had to live.

First, I heard loud and clear from the Universe that my children needed their mother. They needed me to survive. I'd held it all together through Dad's strokes, family food allergies, military moves, and my husband's strokes and brain aneurysm. It was a thin veil of sanity, but I had clung to it tightly those last five years. My babies were curious, bright individuals who had a loving family. If I died, it would break them utterly. I could not have that.

"Breathe, baby. You have to survive this. It's my time now. You have to let me go." These are the words Dad would've said if he wasn't on life support. Every fiber of my being knew I had to let him go, and yet, I fought. I fought for his life, fought for the staff to tell me the truth rather than give me some run around excuse for why he couldn't breathe on his own. I fought to fight because THAT I could handle. I'd fought to live before. I'm a survivor, I told myself.

I'm not someone who gives up though. I fight for my friends. I fight for justice and equality. I fight for love. Survivors know how to fight. Relaxing, on the other hand, is much harder.

When you're faced with the blatant reality that stress could literally kill you right now, not tomorrow, all the lies you tell yourself to feel safer get stripped away. Mine did, anyway. The feeling of my blood rushing through my arteries was so loud. My breath was loud. Every sound was a freight train barreling down the tracks. After five years, that moment, that Friday night at 7:32 PM, I watched the sun setting in the quietly loud room, realizing I had to choose.

Choose right now, in this second between life and death. Not between survival and death, but **life**. What's the difference between surviving and living? Any trauma survivor can tell you coping mechanisms arise when the unexpected and scary happens. They often won't tell you though. That exposes the soft underbelly of the trauma. To most, they look like incredibly strong, maybe even inspiring people.

How we deal with things in the aftermath comes to define us. As the sun set, I knew my blood pressure made me a high risk for stroke. What would it cost me if the fight was more important than anything? Sitting there alone in that room, I knew it would cost me the privilege of watching my children grow up. I would miss their whole lives if I decided to keep fighting the inevitability of Dad's death. I had to accept what I could not change. Reality hit home so very deeply in that moment.

After everything we'd survived, I now had to say goodbye to my dad. Breathe in, breathe out. Feel the truth. The ugly cry came then. I cried until I couldn't cry anymore. I cried for the past, present, and the changed future. And then I dried my eyes, got back up, put on a smile for my children, and went to finish the game with the family.

Zafi, who is a second mother to me, said that morning I needed to disconnect and detach from the stress. She said I needed to do something that had absolutely nothing to do with what was going on with Dad. At first, I was upset. It felt like a betrayal of my father somehow. The more distance I have from that time period however, the more I realize she was right. I trusted her.

We sat down together the four of us, my son, daughter and husband and played a board game. We each got cards and had to complete the railway from one city to the next on our cards for points. Breathe in, breathe out. *You can do this,* I told myself. Their smiles brought me such joy that I was able to be there at the game table playing with them. Being present is remarkably challenging in the face of stress. When the game was done, they of course joyously cried, "Another please!" As I looked at their beaming faces, I realized it had worked. Some of the pressure I felt was less. My blood pressure must've gone down, and my breathing had slowed.

Some people believe there are more bad days than good. However, I believe the moments of joy aren't just fleeting. They are why we get back up and take that next step. Sometimes they hold us deeply and dearly in a sacred space. That Friday night game was sacred.

Surrender to Live

Where is the miracle in this moment? That Friday night because of Zafi's love I was able to detach from five years of stress which had culminated in that moment. Before this leg of the journey was over, I would have to detach a million times more. Even in the detachment process there can be freedom.

A word of caution here: detachment and dissociation are very different things. Dissociation as defined by Merriam-Webster is

> 1. The act or process of dissociating: the state of being dissociated: such as
> a: the process by which a chemical combination breaks up into simpler constituents
> b: the separation of whole segments of the personality (as in dissociative identity disorder) or of discrete metal processes (as in schizophrenia) from the mainstream consciousness or of behavior
> (Merriam-Webster, s.v. "Dissociation")

Merriam-Webster states the definition of detachment as "the action or process of detaching: SEPARATION." (Merriam-Webster, s.v. "Detachment")

Zafi used the term much like my dad did repeatedly. Zafi knew what I didn't even fully recognize at the time. She saw how close to the abyss I was. She wanted me to spend some time doing something **other** than advocating for my father and being swept away in the stress of it all. She was not suggesting I should not care about my father, or that the advocating was not important. Zafi did not want me to disassociate from my life, or myself. She wanted me to be fully present

---

Note: Merriam-Webster, s.v. "Dissociation," accessed February 28, 2023, https://www.merriam-webster.com/dictionary/survivor
Merriam-Webster, s.v. "Detachment," accessed February 28, 2023, https://www.merriam-webster.com/dictionary/survivor

with my children and husband. In order to be fully present and do the hard things in front of me, I needed to play games too. Self-care is far more important than most people realize. For a fleeting moment, my panicked heart felt it was a possible lack of caring to think about anything else. I let that fear-soaked thought slide away and kept bringing myself back to the present and my quest to connect Seattle with New York in our board game. A smile crossed my weary lips, and I knew that Dad would be proud.

That Friday night game night was one of the most important I've ever played. Yes, it's true that in the face of adversity I did not fold. When called to advocate for someone I loved, I was his champion. The importance of that advocacy cannot be undersold. However, it was the light in their eyes and the smiles on their faces that gave me strength to endure. With each laugh, I could feel my blood pressure lowering. I was quite literally taking a breath and refreshing my soul.

Sometimes miracles and overcoming adversity happens in quiet spaces, in the quiet moments—one step at a time. My journey is no different than one step at a time. Yet, I cannot tell you how many times people have said to me they cannot believe that I am even remotely normal' after even just one of the events in my life. The quiet moments of prayer between my husband's healing and my Father's death were my turning points. My Father's death was both an end and a beginning.

My dad had been **my** why for most of my life. We played together when I was a child. My dad took me to Jupiter in the rocking chair with the wicker seat he had as a boy. His father carefully painted that chair in the 1940s. Dad gently held onto the back of the chair as I sat in the pilot's seat eagerly. He made all the noises of the rocket ship and carefully illustrated the moon and each planet we passed on our mission. He finished each such trip by saying I could be anything I chose to be in this lifetime if I believed and worked hard enough. He was my daddy. He showed me what boundaries were when others did not. He protected me when I felt no one else would. He was my tether to the world. I felt like I belonged because I had my dad. We were an odd sort of tribe. We didn't follow conventional rules. That didn't matter. We always had each other. I had taken solace in my father's unwavering love. I could hide from the bad things because Daddy would protect me. I didn't have to get over it, admit anything, or change. Until it was his time. What then?

I immediately looked at my role as a mother. Partly to honor my father's lifelong quest for inner healing, I chose to grow. I could see my whole life play out if I continued as I had. I saw the ripple effect that my own lack of healing could have on my children. They deserved more.

So how do you find optimism or carve it out when things look bleak? How do you find the sun when it seems like all you feel or see is the rain? I cannot tell you the exact path that will work for you. I can tell you the tender moments of love and joy I've experienced that lifted me up each and every step of the way.

We all have moments where we don't want to share things. We all have a soft underbelly we would prefer to hide even if it requires a corset. The truth I have found is that when you take off that corset the underbelly is still there. We all have a choice to either let the past hunt us and color everything we do or to create joy in new moments and new memories. I choose joy.

Sometimes bad things happen to good people. When my dog ate my wooden back massager toy; I didn't have the heart to throw it away. Immediately, I called Dad. He replied with his kind heart and lightning quick wit.

"Bad things happen to good people." He said kindly. I wrote that phrase down in red on blue construction paper and hung it up on a shelf with the chewed-up toy. For years I would walk by the little Ziploc bag and see that sign "bad things happen to good people" and smile. The low times may always be there, but as my coach Dyanne Joyner says "we don't have to live in the shadows". This book is a journey of discovering, carving out and creating the light deliberately and with purpose.

One day, my mentor shared a story from her own mentor. She told my mentor that people who chose to live near the volcano fascinated her. I realized when she said it, that I was in the business of packing up and moving away from the volcano while writing. The book was my moving truck and map away from the volcano.

We don't always have a choice about every circumstance in our lives. At some point, that blessed day of choice inevitably comes. Perhaps you will see your own road map and moving truck of what's possible when you don't have to fight anymore.

This story begins with the hidden away places. We all have stuff. We all have stories. Mine circled around death and mortality for far too long. Intertwined within the hard times were beautiful protective canopies of love. The love endured all things. The love endured heartache, the death of my parents, the unknown of my husband's health, and even my own.

To surrender to live, one must first buy into the concept of surrender. I had to see the value, the absolute necessity of that, in some cases. Accepting that my dad was dying required me to surrender to the truth. It was his time to go, whether I liked it or not. I didn't have to be happy he was dying. It happened independent of my feelings on the matter. I surrendered. The tears washed down my cheeks. I released what there was to let go of. I grieved. I continued to love him anyway, dead or alive.

There came a time when all my defenses were stripped away. A moment punched me in the gut and would not be ignored. Saying goodbye to my dad was such a crossroads. It was time to look behind the door. It was time to heal. What started the day he died was my journey of love, expansion, holding on, and letting go.

I don't have a magic roadmap. My story is one of overcoming adversity, finding my own soul fire, and learning how to heal. It has been a delicate balance of yin and yang, dark and light. I warn you; the journey isn't always pretty. Growth is not always comfortable. Growth can be messy and painful. It has been through searching through my own private rubbish bin that I have been able to be free, one breath at a time.

Every person surrounding my dad's death had lessons to learn. Each was personal to the individual and unexpected. I learned how to grieve one of the deepest losses in my life. I learned what surrender to live meant. I learned that surrender wasn't a four-letter word. It wasn't weakness either. Surrendering, even though it was against my grain, gave me the ability to live.

My story is one of overcoming adversity, finding my own soul fire, and learning how to heal. It has been a delicate balance of yin and yang, dark and light. It has been through searching through my own private rubbish bin that I have been able to be free, one breath at a time.

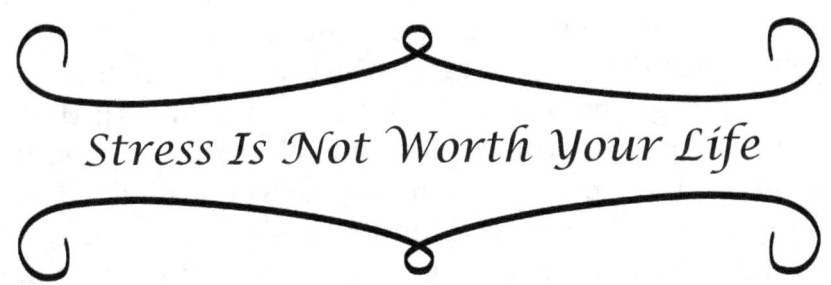

Stress Is Not Worth Your Life

I didn't ask for the bad things to happen. I didn't ask for any of it. So how could I have anything to do with the situation at all?

I was in danger of letting the stress consume me entirely when I lost Dad. After everything I had been through, it felt like this was the thing I could not handle. I didn't want to handle it. I wanted my father to live. I didn't get what I wanted. I had to deal with that.

Stress can kill you. You play a vital role in whether you let it. I have to give up my power and lie down, waiting to die, in order to actually give up on life. My life was waiting for me at the game table. It takes something drastic for stubborn humans, like me, to really buy into that. This concept challenged me. I didn't ask for the bad things to happen. I didn't ask for any of it. So how could I have anything to do with the situation at all?

How could my attitude affect anything? What a huge pill to swallow! My ego did not want me to admit I could be wrong. I certainly didn't want to accept the unacceptable.

I reached my breaking point a million times before I lost my dad. Why then, was that **the moment** I couldn't take anymore? He had made me feel safe and loved my whole life, regardless of what happened. Losing that one person I could trust completely, broke down my walls. Drastic changes needed to happen. My whole world altered. That was my truth.

Realizing things need to change takes bravery. That change can take many forms. Many modalities may be applied in these times. If you reach out and find a medical or psychological professional isn't the right fit for you, keep reaching out. We are all human. The mistake I made for a long time was believing that I had to do it all on my own.

Looking at the root of my own stress, I found answers. I didn't always like the answers I found. My belief came from being let down and feeling really unsafe. I didn't tell anyone how much danger I was in as a teen because I mistakenly thought it kept them safe. It served only to keep me alone. How could I not be alone? Share. Tell my truth.

The freedom that came when I realized that reaching out gave me proverbial wings was intense. Trusting anyone can sometimes be challenging. The false belief that I was entirely alone in the world perpetuated the dysfunction. I didn't have to do it all on my own.

I first had to get off my high horse. I had to realize that I was not allowing anyone to love me by not allowing them to contribute to my well-being. By not letting people love me, or suffering in silence, I only hurt myself. Trusting took time. I started slowly, talking with my husband. I quickly realized that sharing my truth could help him when his time to deal with grief came.

Trust took intention. I deliberately shared the things I really didn't want to share. I allowed myself to be picky about my sharing. I carefully selected who, when and where I shared. Each time I wasn't immediately laughed at, crucified, or belittled; I was shocked. I also stood up taller, gained confidence little by little. Sharing really did help!

I could breathe easier when I took care of myself. I was completely flabbergasted by that fact. I was a caregiver, a mother, a wife. I hadn't made time to care for myself. That wasn't a priority. I came last. Or did I?

Taking care of yourself really does have to come first. It sounds cliché in the airplane when they talk about the oxygen. We often roll our eyes and feel like we're being talked to like children. That doesn't change the absolute truth of it. Without oxygen, you die.

Society often teaches us to give everyone else the oxygen first. Yet, the person who comes to the table without their oxygen mask is oxygen deprived. Trust me, that's not a great place to be. No matter how superhuman you are, what an amazing mother or wife you are, you can't give someone something you do not first have yourself.

The year 2020 became a very charged one. I thought I was doing well saying yes to life, keeping my stress down, and stretching myself into a better human. Curve ball! It was time to learn again. Wait, you mean I have to do more of this learning stuff? Yes. We are constantly being given opportunities to grow and learn. We don't have to like them in order to grow.

As we all sat in the social distance, quarantine 2020 hell we called reality, we all wanted this nightmare to end. We didn't want to get COVID and die, did we? Of course not. We wanted to truly **live** again. As sure as I sat in this hard chair typing until my fingers were cold and numb, this pandemic would end. Science would prevail and find answers for us that were real, sound, and safe. We would open schools again, be able to volunteer, to see the smiles of our children again, go to garden clubs, the bar, chess tournaments, and whatever else sparked our interest. So, here was God's two-by-four therapy, the 2020 pandemic hitting us all over the head with a total reset and reboot. We didn't ask for it. Things happened that we could not control. Every. Single. Day.

They say quarantine time is like dog years. One day was a year though in quarantine time. How did I survive without going mad? Personally, I maintained a small, authentic, inspiring group of friends, and a real community. We took social distancing walks as moms, while the kids played social distancing tic tac toe on the sidewalk. We talked on the phone and the children had video chats. We made excuses to have dates, aka grocery runs, in masks. We still built each other up and worked towards tomorrow, knowing it **would** come. We didn't see it, or feel it with our hands, but we had faith that tomorrow would come. This pandemic would eventually come to a close.

I owed it to my family and more importantly to myself to live a great life. This is true even, and especially in a pandemic. I deserved to be happy. I deserved to be loved like the queen or king I was born to be. You may say, *you can say that, but you're the author of a book, right?* At the time, I was a photographer, stay-at-home mom, president of a school volunteer organization, and garden club member who had not currently authored a book.

My circumstances, from health, my mother's death, to the promise of tomorrow being taken from all of us; I felt deeply powerfully called to write. I was living into my future as an author one day at a time. I had faith I was doing something meaningful. I could always see to the other side of my personal brick walls. Faith is what helped me to know that there was solid ground on the other side. This type of faith was trust in the process and in the dream.

Stress will come. Sometimes it was so heavy that I didn't know if I could take another breath of air. It could be the stress of a death, my husband's stroke, or more traumatizing like an act of violence. When things were that big, I dealt in moments. I chose who I wanted to be one at a time. I realized that those small moments built up to something larger. They added up to make days and weeks where I did get through seemingly insurmountable things. I blinked and weeks had turned into years. The tough times gave way to better, happier ones.

It may take time to gather yourself. That's okay. That's normal.

You can choose to float on the sea of life and let the stress carry you away. There are times we all need to circle the drain emotionally to see the way out. It happens faster than we can take a breath. Sometimes, we lie back and ride that sea so far that we end up countries away and have absolutely no clue how to get back. I've been there, too. When you're ready, and find a calm shore, then growth is ready for you.

Cutting to the chase, when Dad died, I wasn't ready to lose him. He'd had his abdominal aortic aneurysm replaced with fresh aorta but lost six liters of blood on the table. After living with five years of constant fight or flight, my body was addicted to cortisol, also known as the stress hormone. This hormone is released at times of stress, and after five years of constant exposure my body was used to always being 'on' and being hyper-aware. Yes, that's a thing, unfortunately. I realized I could feel my pulse in my aorta and up both sides of my neck in my carotid arteries. I knew my blood pressure was dangerously high, stroke high. I knew that if I didn't take Zafi's advice and unplug from that stress, my family would bury me too.

I had no clue how to do "unplug". One breath at a time I decided that stress was not worth my life. I was not willing to lose my family, or the ability to watch my babies grow up. That stopped me in my tracks. I stood up in that sea of my life and began walking towards the shore. Each and every one of my experiences have shaped and carved me like the Grand Canyon.

Stress Is Not Worth Your Life

The thing is, at some point, you do get to be the sculptor of your own life. You choose in each moment what's important, even if subconsciously. Sometimes choosing requires your own two-by-four. Other times, it's a single step. Then, another. And another.

I stopped being willing to allow my fear to run every decision or non-decision in my life. I became unwilling to allow it that level of control any longer. I chose to systematically undo the programming of fear and hiding in the shadows of my life.

It's not been easy work. I still shake with unbridled fear at ridiculous things. I've chastised myself for it, belittled myself for it, you name it. Until I took charge of my own emotions, I did not see truths in front of my face. I didn't see how every micro-decision had fed that fear-based mentality and protection mechanism. Don't get me wrong, I've been through some stuff, as you may say. I was just **finally** unwilling to choose life in the same way as I'd always done.

Choosing newly for me required that someone grabbed my tiny boat before it fell off Niagara Falls. Then they held up the mirror. Zafi showed me how close I was to the precipice from which I could not return. I was a bear about it all. I also listened to her sage advice.

I am not done with my self-work on this topic. I have "miles to go before I sleep", as Robert Frost said in "Stopping By Woods on a Snowy Evening." That poem has sustained me through many dark times. If you're alive, you can still learn. That's my motto. If your willing heart can feel the light, even though you are afraid or sad. Then, you have the ability to be more tomorrow than you are today.

My friend constantly cautions me that leaning on other people for one's happiness is very dangerous. He's right of course. However, I postulate, once you have found some balance for yourself, community is a beloved, amazing thing. Most people avoid leaning on others like the plague. I've been one of them. However, I'm not talking about making another person responsible for your happiness in a codependent way. I'm speaking of living in community with people who help inspire you, listen to you and have you feel that sense of belonging. There's great value in a community of friends who are there to support each other. Community is much more than where your house is situated. Community can be a thriving ecosystem of love.

When the shutdown happened, I was fully immersed in my life. Yet, there was very little time for me, personally. I was on three boards and in four organizations. I was (and am) a wife, a mother of two children and three fur babies, and a photographer. I put myself out there more building the business. I loved volunteering at the school and the garden club. Still, I held back parts of my soul. I pushed so much for everyone and everything else, that I did not take time for myself.

The shutdown in my home state was in March of 2020 and Mom's metastatic lung cancer diagnosis was delivered the same week. I quickly realized I'd go mad if I didn't change my frame of mind and take time for me. So, I created the social distancing walks with my friend Lisa and our children. They wore masks so they could just be kids and play pretend. We talked, walked and created listening space. There were also many other things I did solo of course, including writing and gardening.

Stress Is Not Worth Your Life

Mom's diagnosis hit us all like a ton of bricks, even if I pretended it didn't. I didn't lie to Mom per se, but I knew she needed strength and listening from me as well as love and being present. Each day, I did what I needed to whether it was dance, gardening, or what have you in order to be 'her rock' because she needed that. Cultivating self-care became more of a pattern in order to help her. I saw the value. I could let go of the feeling that it was selfish if I looked at it that way. Every day required something different. I made allowances for it all.

Time is so very fleeting, and as many have said, you don't regret what you have done nearly as much as what was left undone. This statement applies to many areas of our lives. With Mom, I knew time wouldn't pass like quarantine time. I knew it was a shooting star. I chose to grab on and spend each moment I could, authentically and with love.

Mom and I did a lot of healing our relationship together. The resulting gift we were given was being present in each moment we had together. Meanwhile, she was on fifteen liters of oxygen per minute, using the suction tool because the tumor was preventing her breathing, and opening the nearby artery. Without another single thought in my head, I was able to make her coffee, knowing that she may only have the strength for one or two sips. She smiled because the kindness touched her. She told me her heart, her lessons learned, and her undone moments.

I bore witness to a woman who had been given nothing and yet made a pretty great life all on her own. She did the business of her life's work and left no skeletons in her closet. As I told her then, I have one in mine, but he's a Halloween decoration. She laughed, and so did I. Another miracle.

Stress could have stolen all joy from me and my mother. No one would have blamed us. We would have missed out on all the catching up we had to do. We didn't miss one precious second. We witnessed it all.

When it was all over, I asked myself important questions. *How old are you now? What's more, what have you learned? Are your choices more meaningful and thought out these days?*

I discovered that I liked family game night. I learned how to let go with grace. I found out that I could be bigger than my fear, but it was a choice I'd have to continue to make. I discovered that lowering stress wasn't some pointless gimmick. My life was important to me. I wanted to be the best mom I could, but in order to pull that off I'd have to take on stress management skills. Stress wasn't worth my life. Having more time watching my babies grow meant the world to me. I was up for the task.

The mistake I made for a long time was believing that I had to do it all on my own.

The Door I Wasn't Willing to Walk Through

In order to live fully, I first have to be willing to let go of past wounds. It all begins with willingness.

Some people tell me that I've been through an awful lot in my life. I'm sure there are plenty of people who've been through more than I have. The Universe's two-by-four therapy has slowly but surely taught me that fear is a liar and must be evicted from running my life to truly live. In order to live fully, I first have to be willing to let go of the past wounds. It all begins with willingness.

The fear may always be there. In spite of the shaking, I am brave. Despite the lie that my lizard brain tells me, **there is no dinosaur coming to eat me.** This saying of Zafi's has gotten me through more than I can say. I may shake when a stranger walks by me without knowing why. I still get to choose who to be in each moment. I can look around, see that there are no dinosaurs, and choose to say hello.

What follows is the door I was unwilling to walk through. These are the things I was too scared to say or admit to even myself. When my father died, I saw that door again. It was ten feet tall, hard, cold, made of steel, and encased in lead. The opportunity came knocking to deal with the old trauma. This time, I chose differently. Turning the skeleton key in the lock, I opened that door and walked through, back in time. My hope is that through sharing my experiences with raw honesty, you can see a different way to walk through your own doors.

My parents separated when I was eleven and my mom started dating a few years later. She found someone she thought was attractive and charming. She asked my opinion of him. Why had she listened to me back at the very beginning when she met him? I was a fourteen-year-old child who had no idea what he was capable of then. Back then I wore size fourteen jeans

The Door I Wasn't Willing to Walk Through

and men's XL flannels (which were far too large) under the guise of the grunge look, but I wasn't a stoner by any means. At the time, I was head over heels in love with my first boyfriend, who loved grunge music. Mom treated us to a trip to the vice-based business the guy she was dating owned, in order to introduce us. All I saw in mom's new boyfriend was his smile and the business he owned. I was naïve. I thought that everyone was good. She could have told me it had rained skittles and I would've believed it then.

There was a lot behind that smile. All too quickly, reality slapped me in the face. Nightmare Man, as I will call him, was a drug dealer. He tried to hide that and lie about it, like everything else. So how do I know? A year before they got married, his car was impounded for cocaine possession. "It wasn't mine" he said. In the same breath, he asked my mother to help him steal his car out of the impound for him. She broke up with Nightmare Man when that happened. I discovered it wasn't the first time he'd been stopped for cocaine possession.

They were broken-up for several months, until Christmas came, and he spouted some sob story my mom took to heart and decided to believe that he would change. He eventually proposed and my mom said yes. Before summer vacation that school year, someone at school asked me about the guy my mom was engaged to. When I told her his name, fear crossed her eyes, and she stopped dead in her tracks. "He sold drugs to Nate," she said. "He's bad news, Sarah!" "I know he is." I responded, helpless to change the outcome.

My mom wouldn't listen to me. I wanted to kick myself. Why did my voice matter when I didn't know any better? Why didn't it matter when I found out he was dangerous? What kind of alternate universe had I landed myself in? I tried talking to Mom. I tried reasoning with her. She married him anyway.

Knock, knock, knock! I stirred my sleepy teenage head and woke to the sound of the fervent knock at the door. A quick look at the clock told me that it was late. It was September again and I was late for school! I pulled on fresh clothes, rushed to the door and told my dear friend and neighbor, Ivy, that I'd be right out. I ran into the bathroom and washed my face and brushed my teeth simultaneously, all the while scolding myself for not getting up earlier. Almost as if there were the angel and devil on my shoulder, my adult self said *I should've gone to bed earlier.* My inner child said *but I wasn't tired then.*

"Catch up!" She said.

"I'm sorry I'm late," I said. Together we ran to the bus stop by the road. We made it just as the bus pulled up.

That day was to be one of my last times going to the bus stop. In the blink of an eye, my stepfather took us away from our hometown, my safe haven. My mother let him. He said he didn't like the nosy neighbors. The truth is he didn't like that he couldn't do whatever he wanted without someone knowing. He moved us to a small, white trailer forty minutes from my old home. My new bedroom door didn't even shut all the way, let alone lock.

Beep, beep, beep went my alarm, cold and menacingly. I arose wide awake and alert. I couldn't be caught off guard here. It wasn't safe. With all the efficiency that Ivy wished I had, I got up alone and on time. No knock on the door would come. Mom and I got into the sky-blue four door sedan quietly. Even the car

The Door I Wasn't Willing to Walk Through

door shutting was loud. Silence. Silence was loud.

"Nightmare Man wants you to transfer to school here," she said after a very pregnant pause. *I bet he does,* I thought. *He wants me totally alone in the world.* I remembered the timeline of the past few months. At the beginning of September they got married at a park wearing white cowboy hats and jeans. Two days later, I started school. I was finally used to it there after my parents' separation. It felt normal. I was home there. I had a home there. Not even a month had gone by before he wanted us to move to his house. He called it a house?! It was a torture chamber on a desert island for me. By November, my father moved to Georgia, states away. *Now he wants to take me out of school,* I thought. I'd be dead for sure.

"Did you hear me? Sarah?"

"I heard you, Mom. I'm not changing schools. I'm not leaving dance. If you make me do that; I'm moving down to Georgia with Dad." She responded with silence.

The trees were bare, and it was winter again. The wind whipped the tiny snowflakes around in swirls across the barren fields. Long dead corn stalks barely popped their heads up from the pristine white snow. Looking out the window of that blue car, my mother's dream come true car, you would have thought it picturesque. That day though, and many others like it, as we drove into school, it felt like a barren wasteland and worlds away from my life. My life was forty minutes away by car. He wanted me to stop going to my school. He wanted me to be seen and not heard.

Nightmare Man wanted a lot of things, but my mother wasn't one of them. He didn't love her. He wanted the child support money that she got from my father weekly. He convinced her that she was terrible with money and should give it all to him to manage. She did as he asked. He needed supplies for his business, and she gave him every penny of my college savings. As part of the Divorce agreement, my dad gave mother half of his 401K retirement money. It was to be used only for my college tuition. At that time, it would've easily paid my way through most four year schools anywhere in the country. It was quite literally my ticket to the future.

Like a silent deadly thief, he chipped away at my mother's will. "She won't get into college anyway," he said. "She'll never amount to anything," he said. "I need it now and can pay you back later." Just like that, there it went. Nightmare Man wanted that $25,000. He got it.

We got an I.O.U. paper signed at the bank. It had to be official right? Mom tried to convince me that it was for the best, and that he would give it back. I knew that he never would. He married my mom in early September and by December, he'd gotten rid of my dog, my cat, my home, our home phone; and he'd gotten his hands on my college savings and every other penny we had. Good lord, where was the light?

As we got to school that morning, I quietly thanked my mother for the ride. She wasn't happy with me for saying I wouldn't go to a different school. The rides were long into school. That took something for her to manage.

"He'll kill me if I leave the places where people know me," I said, "He's an abuser. He wants us to be alone. He already got us away from the friends and neighbors who loved us. If I say yes to you, he'll get it all. Going to Georgia would be a lot easier than dying, Mom." I got out of the car and went to school.

The Door I Wasn't Willing to Walk Through

Each step I took felt like my own personal freedom march. I had stood up for myself. I couldn't care if someone thought I was spoiled. I had to survive. I took a deep breath, left that conversation outside the building, and walked in.

I had worked out every single time that I would have to be alone with Nightmare Man. Everything he ever said about or to me was negative or demeaning and he was constantly angry and drank every night. I never wanted to discover what would happen if my mother wasn't standing between us as a buffer to his unbridled rage. In an effort to stay alive, I made certain that I was never in that position, if I could help it. So, on occasion I spent the night at my boyfriend, Jeremy's house. As a teenager in high school, you can imagine that this elicited a myriad of moral questions from my peers and, most probably, their families as well. What they didn't know, is that I was trying to simply survive. I could not be alone with my stepfather because I feared that, with no one looking, he would kill me. So, I endured the laughs and snickers on the mornings that I got on the bus at his house.

"Would you like me to make you a coffee, Baby?" Jeremy asked.

"Yes, please," I replied very groggily. "Thank you."

"I have your favorite cup," he said. There, on the counter sat my large bright pink insulated coffee mug. It was conveniently located next to the toaster and the box of cinnamon pastries. Without even asking, he popped two pastries for each of us. Each first bite was always the best. I would close my eyes and let the cinnamon sweetness engulf my senses.

"Nectar of the Gods," I gushed as I gratefully sipped the warm, sweet, creamy, chocolaty drink. Somewhere deep down it was coffee. That day though, it was pure joy.

You see, Jeremy loved me when I saw love nowhere else. He courted me for months before we began dating. As time went on, he proved himself kind and gentle. I fell for the sweetness in his heart and for the way he saw me as much as the love he made me believe was real.

We got off the bus at school after passing the farms and the trees and had a little time before classes began. "Let's go down to the band wing," I said.

"You're not gonna make me learn to play the flute, are you?" Jeremy replied with a smile.

"No," I laughed, "I just don't want to sit in the cafeteria with everyone looking at me."

Without another word his long warm fingers grabbed my hand, and we walked in silence. It was always deserted in the band wing at that time of day and there weren't any other classrooms nearby, only the auditorium. We would lean against the sand-colored brick wall enjoying the mocha and the warm pastries if we had any left after the bus ride. This was one example where the smallest act of kindness ended up being the biggest.

Jeremy loved me when I could not love myself. He loved me when I was depressed. He loved me when I did not see a light anywhere. He loved me even though I was so terrified that I slept with a knife in my hand out of fear for my own safety every single night. He loved me anyway. It seemed weird, how could I be loved unconditionally by one person and hated by another.

At the beginning of the school year, I asked him if he would come to the dance studio with me. I had done ballet, jazz, tap, and pointe or some combination thereof most of my life. He stared at me as if I had just asked him to run naked through the school. "You mean you want me to put on tights or a tutu?" He asked.

I laughed, "That would be hilarious, but no you won't have to wear a tutu. Guys don't wear a tutu. They do wear tights though. We had a guy in the studio in past years and he danced with April. It was amazing! I promise it isn't a girly thing. Besides, think of all the girls in leotards." I'm sure that the last thing he really wanted to do was learn ballet. But learn he did. That was love.

"Hey Baby," I said. "Do you like Shakespeare?"

"What do you mean, do I like Shakespeare? I guess so."

Seeing the opening I asked "would you take Shakespeare with me? For a senior elective class, Shakespeare exists. When I asked the guidance counselor, they mentioned we had to get ten people to sign up in order to hold the class. Mrs. T said that the class hasn't been held in twenty-five years. I think I'd be awesome to take Shakespeare."

Jeremy went right to work on it with me, lobbying our entire class to sign up for Shakespeare. He liked the challenge of it. In the end, we did get more than ten people to sign up and Shakespeare did happen that year. It was awesome. I don't know if I ever really thanked him properly for helping me.

We had thinkers and philosophers and members of every kind of clique imaginable inside that one class of eleven people. Despite our diverse social identities, we came together to learn what very few in our school system had the opportunity to learn. The play we put on for class was my one and only chance at theater. I loved it. Practicing at the dance studio for five days a week I didn't have any time to join theater. I always wished I could. We didn't even have to perform in front of the school. Interestingly, I was never really that nervous to be seen on stage until after my stepfather married my mother. That was the year my stage fright started.

Each day I counted the seconds until I could get into the art studio. Every chance I got; I chose to stay after school soaking up the marrow of life held within the four walls of the art room. Within the dark, seemingly endless night, they were there. Sculpture and dance gave me a sense of normalcy.

We began sculpture lessons with a tiny thing our teacher, Ms. H, called foam core. We were to make an abstract piece with this foam filled paper and glue. "Push the limits of form and function. See what happens when you do," said our kind, insightful teacher.

I was used to the way she taught after having Studio in Art, where we learned drawing and painting, with her in years past. If sculpture was like this mixture of pins, glue and foam core structure hell, then I wasn't sure I wanted to be part of it. I lovingly spray-painted over my paper piece and made it look like a green stone. It was an amalgamation of sharp jagged pieces with smooth stairs. It was complete.

Thankfully, blissfully, that unit passed as quickly as it came. We had learned the lesson of impermanence and that there are limits to three-dimensional form. Next, we got to begin working with clay. During Studio Art we were introduced to gesture drawings. Gesture drawings are quick, often timed, exercises where the goal is to capture the large shapes of the subject in a loose, free manner. Given such a small amount of time,

The Door I Wasn't Willing to Walk Through

the artist has to make decisions quickly, in order to capture the general idea of the subject and has to forgo concentrating on the details. Much like our gesture drawings, we would do gesture sculptures.

In sculpture class, Jay was up on the table again. No, he didn't get in trouble for it. He was our model. The desks were arranged in a circular fashion as we all had a good, albeit slightly different view of Jay. He was older than I was. This was one of two times a day I saw him. Later in the afternoon, he'd be at the dance studio dancing with April. He liked making me work harder and wore the clothes with the most folds. "I have to make it fun for you," he'd say.

Some say that artists come in mainly one form or another. Some are more at home and at ease with two-dimensional work and others with sculpture. I had been critical of my drawings and my lines. The perfectionist worked its way out of my skin like a snake. It slithered its way into my soul and told me that my lines weren't right. Glancing at the papers of other people in the room it always compared my work to theirs. Then we touched clay.

Ms. H gave us each our very own bag of stoneware clay. The mocha-colored rectangular block retained the wrinkles from the plastic bag as we unsheathed it from its home. We each put our blocks on the table as instructed and waited. As soon as I touched the cool moist medium, I was entranced. She gave us time to carve out the big shapes of the boy on the table. He sat in a chair, crossing one leg over the other, leaning on that top leg. His nineties grunge style plaid flannel folded all around him.

The whole world melted away when I touched the clay. There was only the task at hand, my tools, and the light streaming in from the windows. Looking back, it was mindfulness training. I had no clue at the time. We carved the big blocks into a human form and slowly worked our way to the details. The inner perfectionist was nowhere to be seen. My inner child got to play here. It **was** like playing in the mud, with purpose. When we were introduced to the slip bucket, I realized that it was playing in the mud. Ms. H described how the clay got dug up, purified, and sent to us. When we threw our scraps into the slip bucket, we recycled the earth literally. It landed with a wet plop into the opaque tan water. I couldn't help but touch that very wet bit sticking out on top. It squished between my fingers with such satisfaction and ease. I was home here. **This** was my home. No critics. No stepfathers. No worries. No death. Just creation.

A few gesture sculptures later, we moved on to the larger hollow built slab construction. This would be a challenge for us and somewhat reminiscent of our time with the dreaded foam core. We would quickly find the limits of the clay, how the moisture would change it, and how important techniques like slipping and scoring would be.

The assignment was to make a human figure. We had time to think with our sketchpad. Sketching just stressed me out quite frankly. She gave us an oil-based modeling clay and tools. I sculpted a small bust of a man. Then, we got to roll out the clay slabs on the canvas with the roller and set to work. I brought my board to the table with my slab of clay and formed the shape of the base. She taught us how to slip and score the edges of the slabs, to join two pieces as one. With the precision of a surgeon, I used the needle tool to cut the clay bottom. I thought I was beginning just below

The Door I Wasn't Willing to Walk Through

the butt of a man. When Ms. H came over and looked at the shapes I'd made, she noted how he looked very much like a feminine form.

How can I do this without seeing anyone? Seeing a model on the table made it easier somehow. The teacher handed me a twelve inch mirror and directed me to the paint closet.

"I'm not allowed to give you naked figure models because you're underage," she said kindly, "You are well within your rights to take this mirror and look at yourself with this door closed for privacy of course."

Horrified, I stared at the mirror, "You mean, look at **myself**?"

"Yes, Bundeuker," she said gently. She always had made up pet names for all her students.

Over the coming months, I would visit the closet when I got stumped with the piece. I stripped away my teenage discomfort and just saw as an artist would. It was perhaps the first time I'd seen myself through the eyes of an artist. The sculpted woman became my salvation during the darkest hours of my life.

Even in the worst times, there was love. There were many ways where people showed me kindness from the art teacher who let me work on extra projects and stay after school almost every day to my boyfriend putting on a pair of white, skintight tights and learning ballet. There were many occasions when people showed me kindness.

Humans can overcome so much more than they think they can. Many things may lend us to being either optimistic or pessimistic. Regardless, the truth is we are each capable of seeing the light, finding the light, and being the light.

Sometimes light will manifest in ways we may not expect, however.

Soul Fire

Clear, bright light illuminated the kitchen, an afront to how I felt. I sat on the red kitchen carpet, knife in hand, feeling hopeless, pondering my life. Should I live? Logic won out as I weighed the pros and cons. Suddenly and sharply, like the large knife in my hand, I realized that Nightmare Man would win if I took my own life. Again, I said to myself that he was not worth it. He didn't deserve to win. Those were my conscious thoughts.

Unconsciously, I looked for a way out, desperately craving it. I knew that people loved me. My dad loved me. My friends, family and my boyfriend loved me. I would be missed. I closed my eyes with the fresh image of the blood red kitchen carpet I sat on burned into my retinas. Seriously, who puts carpet in a kitchen? The sun lit up my eyelids and warmed me, even though it was cold outside. My woman. She wasn't finished. My clay creation of life was incomplete. I was incomplete. I still had art. I had dance.

In these two spaces, I had the freedom to be. I was an artist. I was a soul worthy of love, worthy of life. When I danced and sculpted, I didn't have to explain my existence. I did not have to explain how I felt. Nightmare man had taken control of so much of my life, yet through art and dance, I could completely express myself from the tips of my toes to my fingertips. I chose again. I chose in that moment on that red kitchen carpet with the sun streaming in on me. I was a survivor. I would live and thrive and do well. The evil would not swallow me whole.

That moment was the hardest I'd been through up until that point. Ever since, I have faced demons of different varieties. Yet, almost instinctively, I chose to live. I birthed the woman. She stood without arms or

The Door I Wasn't Willing to Walk Through

legs around fifteen inches tall and six and a half inches wide. When she was complete, the deep darkness subsided.

Don't get me wrong. There were days that I had to claw my way out. There were days where I didn't see any hope. I deliberately inserted life in the ways that sustained me, even when I didn't feel like it.

Per the terms of the divorce, visitation was set at every other weekend with Dad. When he moved to Georgia, I got to go down there for the whole Christmas break. A northerner in the south for Christmas is definitely a vacation! Dad helped me relish in it too. Bless him! Growing up, we had white dishes that had black ornate flowers and a black rim around each plate. Dad got them in the divorce. They came with water goblets. They had a fancy black exterior with a pristine white interior and thin stems. Dad set up the tiny balcony in his apartment in Columbus, Georgia for Christmas breakfast. He set the black tablecloth and napkins out as if we were eating in the finest restaurant in the world. He even got out the water goblets and filled them with orange juice. He made us pancakes, his specialty for breakfast. The breeze wasn't even cool enough to need a jacket as it was seventy-five degrees out that day.

We had stopped a few days prior on the side of the road where a lovely elderly man was selling authentic bonsai trees. I picked out the biggest, most beautiful thitry year-old juniper tree. It had a rectangular pot with rocks and plenty of drainage. We hung a few tiny objects we called ornaments on the juniper. It was lovingly placed on Dad's wooden coffee table. He'd made it himself in the 1970s. It had a raw sienna aged patina and a touch of polyurethane.

"Get the plates please," Dad said as he was finishing the pancakes on the stove. I set them down gently and watched what he was doing. I was going to make each moment in heaven count. When breakfast was ready, we joined our orange juice goblets and took our plastic lawn chair seats with our pancakes and scrambled eggs. The sun peeked around the apartment building and warmed the back of my head. He smiled and squinted some as the sun went through his glasses to his hazel eyes. It was so good to see him.

"Thanks, Dad. This is beautiful and so yummy," I said.

"You're welcome, Sweet Baby," he said. I took a deep breath in, relishing the clean warm air in my nostrils and closed my eyes. This was love. It was real.

While visiting Dad in Georgia, we took a short drive down to Destin, Florida. We parked his gold station wagon and walked to the sands. I took off my shoes as soon as we stopped. When my feet hit the pavement, it was cool to the touch. The sand tickled my feet and gently massaged them as we walked arm in arm to the water's edge. The sight of the pure white sands and mint green crystal-clear water took my breath away. It was so gorgeous! Looking left and right, there was only one couple to be seen, other than Dad and I. For as far as the eye could see, the sands were pure white. You could see into the water, below the surface for what seemed like forever. That was my first experience with that type of water and with the Gulf of Mexico. I was in love instantly.

Dad and I walked and talked about school, boys, his new job learning COBOL and many other things. He told me how a puddle froze one day. "It shut down the entire building. Everyone went out to catch a glimpse of

The Door I Wasn't Willing to Walk Through

the ice. They had never seen it before," he laughed his big, hearty belly laugh then. His straight teeth gleamed from the sun and he tipped his head back a bit. "Can you imagine never seeing water freeze," he said laughing.

Before long the couple walking along the water's edge reached where we had stopped. They started chatting us up and asking if we were locals. Only locals usually went there that time of year. When we explained that we were visitors, they told us about how close the dolphins come in March to feed on the fish that school there. Dad asked the couple if they recommended a great place to eat nearby. "The Red Bar is great," said the man, "It's not too far up the way and has great food." Dad and I thanked them and slowly walked towards the car. We promised them that we'd try to come back in the Springtime to see the dolphins in their glory.

I could hardly believe my eyes as we pulled up to the place. Yep, it was actually called the Red Bar. Dad hadn't had a drink in eight years at that point. He wouldn't usually go to a place that even served alcohol, let alone one that called itself a bar. He was very dedicated to not drinking. He also had OCD (obsessive compulsive disorder) and had a lot of rules as a result. Dad said he was ok to go in when I asked him though.

I remember the red décor everywhere when we went in and the clean wooden tables. The waitress excitedly and a bit sadly told us that we had just missed Jim Carrey. "They just finished filming The Truman Show here yesterday," she said, "He came in all the time while they were here though." I sat back and got more comfortable in my seat. *Wow, movie royalty may have sat in this seat! How cool is that?*

I came back from that visit with Dad a very different person than I had been when I left. Having a break from someone who terrified me on a continual and constant basis made me realize that there was an actual real life **outside** of what he created. Visiting Dad reminded me that I mattered, and the terrible things Nightmare Man said were wrong. Very importantly, I realized that I could get out. Dad would let me live with him if I wanted. I had a way out of that hell. All I had to do was get As and Bs and I could go to college in-state in Georgia for free to boot! I scarcely could believe it. I clung onto something I hadn't seen in a while as I came back home: hope. I had hope.

One night, a few months later, I'd convinced Mom to spend the night at our old house again. My brother had moved into the house in our absence. I hadn't spent much time with him. Nightmare Man called. Silent as a mouse, I picked up the receiver. I sat on my bed. I had asked my mother to move back to the house that week. Mom was discussing it with him.

"I'd rather take a shotgun to her head and shoot her myself than let her move back there," he said with such bile and hatred that I backed away and hung up. After several long minutes, the phone call ended. I went in to talk to my mother and asked her straight out what he'd said. She didn't tell me. I confessed that I had heard the words he said and asked her again. I asked her what she was going to do.

"His mother is dying. He needs me," she said with sad eyes. The betrayal was more than I could bear. It wasn't the first time he'd hinted at my demise. This time it wasn't even a hint or a veiled threat. It was specific and pointed. It wasn't a fluke, or a slip of the tongue. She didn't defend me. I moved back into my old

The Door I Wasn't Willing to Walk Through

house with my brother the very next day. She went back to him.

Before long, Mom came to visit. He called again. They began fighting almost instantly. This time, she pressed the record button on the phone's answering machine. The mini cassette recorded the conversation. He threatened to kill me again. He said he would follow me to dance and take me into the woods where no one would find me. The bus let me off almost a mile from the dance studio at the end of a dead-end street. One whole side was thick woods, and the other side was lined with houses set far back from the street. I'd never seen neighbors outdoors while walking and as I listened to him threaten me on the recording, I realized he could likely attack me without being seen. He said if I ever had children, he would kill them too. He said a lot of things that abusive people say. This time though, Mom went to get a restraining order. This time, it finally mattered.

The damage was done as far as I was concerned. I was alone. I was expendable. I was unprotected. Other people got protected. The life lesson I took away then was that I had to do it on my own. I had to rely on myself. The survivor was born.

Through the years, I've chosen to share bits and pieces of my story with certain trusted individuals. Most gasp in horror and disbelief. Some can listen for a while. They all usually want to try to find a way to fix it, though. People want to fix the unfixable and find words of comfort, especially in the most unbearable of times. While a pat answer may in fact be quite triggering, the intention is usually good.

Why do I share? I do it for several reasons. First off, the person said something similar that had me know that they needed to hear a piece of the story. Sometimes, I shared because I trusted them and wanted them to know who they were friends with. Honestly, sometimes it was a test. Could they actually handle being my friend? Would they run away once they knew? They never did run, by the way. The survivor in me always thought they would.

Now, I ask myself, why exactly would they run as I laid my most raw, vulnerable moments bare for them as my friend? They didn't. They tried, as best they could to be with the unbearable. They tried to help, console, listen, and sometimes to just hold the silence of empathy. Finally, they usually all said, 'you've been through so much.'

I love my friends dearly. Please believe that. But what does that mean exactly? What is so much? Is there a line past which, most humans do not exceed and survive? Should there be a line? Is there a line past which most humans can't simply be with or listen to? Yes. We are human. We do the best we can.

When I opened the door to my past and walked through, I realized that sharing with people held its own freedom. Each time reminds me that my body is reacting to very old stimuli. Each time I share my truth vulnerably, the fear loses a piece of its power over me.

Walking through that door, exposing that old pain had me look at not only the incidents themselves. I also looked at my own decisions, emotions, and tools I'd had until that point. I saw how much I hid myself away to stay safe. I felt the emotions. I realized what tools I needed to sharpen and what skills needed to be acquired. I had to take responsibility for my life when I walked through the door. I was the one who did not pursue my dreams, not him. I was the one who didn't

The Door I Wasn't Willing to Walk Through

let my art piece go to the art museum in NYC. I was the one who was too afraid to stand out in a crowd, to be seen. I did those things. Not him.

I saw what there was for me to do next. Open up the doors, throw out the trash, and move away from the volcano.

Walking through that door, exposing that old pain had me look at not only the incidents themselves. I had to take responsibility for my life. I was the one who did not pursue my dreams, not him.

Soul Fire

Hiding

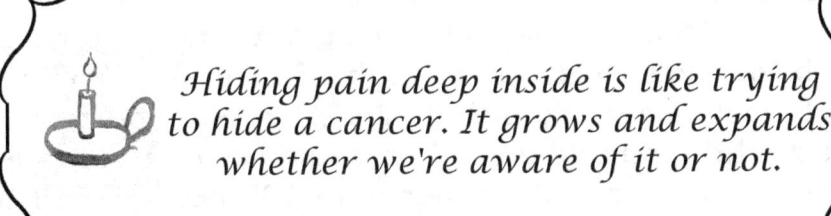

Hiding pain deep inside is like trying to hide a cancer. It grows and expands whether we're aware of it or not.

Soul Fire

Most people hide. They won't tell you they do, or even seem like they are hiding. Most people have a mask they put on in public. That mask may change depending on who they're going to see that day, or what job title they hold. For survivors though, the hiding is so much deeper than that.

The definition of a survivor is: "1. to remain alive or in existence: live on. 2. To continue to function or prosper. (Merriam-Webster, s.v. "Survivor")

People do not have to die for you to feel like a survivor. It could be a traumatic event in which you feared you or someone you love would be harmed. The sad truth is that more of us are survivors than ever before.

Survivors hide so much for so long that they can't remember why. I didn't even realize I did it anymore. I chose subconsciously, on autopilot. It happened so fast that I believed I wanted those things. Years of self-conditioning and coping mechanisms got me there. I had to look at the decisions I was making. I wanted change but had no clue how. I retraced my steps.

Remember, my hiding started with size fourteen jeans and Men's XL flannels. Being a teenager, copying my boyfriend's look was enough of a reason. No one would look deeper than that. Under the size fourteens, I was a 125-pound dancer. You could see every muscle in my body. I was 125 rather than 105 because I also liked to lift weights. Yes, it was an odd combination. Lifting weights, specifically leg pressing made me feel powerful. I had felt what it was to be weak and I no longer wanted to be that. I didn't want people to see my body. I didn't want someone talking to me because they

---

Note: Merriam-Webster, s.v. "Survivor," accessed February 28, 2023, https://www.merriam-webster.com/dictionary/survivor

thought I was pretty. I wanted them to talk to me because of who I was inside. I chose who I let in. Hiding felt safer than being exposed.

When you've had to live in bad circumstances with people who repeatedly violate your sense of safety and your personal space, it changes you. It colors how you perceive everything. I hid for years to protect myself. It took me many years to be able to trust people again, but it's a choice I had to make in order to grow.

Hiding pain deep inside is like trying to hide a cancer. It grows and expands whether we're aware of it or not. For years I'd hidden not only from my stepfather, but I'd also hidden exactly how afraid of him I was from the other people in my life. I even hid my hiding. Even though I was one, I didn't want to be a victim. I didn't want other people to see me as a victim. In my head, if I didn't say I was a victim, then I wasn't one. Back then I thought victims had to be weak. I refused to be weak.

I didn't stay alone like some choose to do after trauma. Sometimes I was able to open my heart fully in a relationship. More often, when I was younger, I chose relationships where I could help in some way. I chose this because it was safer than giving my whole heart and being destroyed when the relationship ended. I hid behind being a fixer in relationships. I cared for them deeply, don't get me wrong. I could not easily open my soft underbelly to them. I kept the corset firmly in place.

Hiding can be much more than not sharing all of yourself with a partner. For me, it was literal as well. After living with my ex-stepfather, I hid my talents and my skills, hoping not to draw too much attention to myself. I was afraid he'd find me and kill me like he said he would.

Soul Fire

Abusive people do very specific things to control you. First, he got rid of my cat and dog. Then, he made us move forty minutes away from people we knew, away from our support system. He shut off our phone. He tried to take me out of dance and my school too. That was the hard line where I held firm. I knew I'd be dead if that happened. There would be no one to miss me if I was a new kid in a new school.

While I did my best to make sure that he'd go to jail if he'd actually killed me when I was a teenager, I also spent the next twenty plus years hiding from any type of spotlight. I stayed quiet, with the familiar pang of fear in my chest and prayed no one would see my scars. My faulty logic told me that if I didn't talk about it, then it didn't happen. I was brave in order to actually survive, and yet I still was hiding. I thought it would fade with time. The survivor inside of me didn't simply stop existing once the trauma stopped. I had to change that pattern myself.

Sometimes, in the darkness, there is light. It could be a friend or even a stranger who shows you a kindness. It could be your love for your craft, hobby or even your career. Writing is incredibly cathartic. When I was a teenager, I wrote a lot. There were some things I was too afraid to write about. Those, of course, were the very things I really needed to express. I hid even within the supposedly safe confines of my writing. Even that didn't feel safe because he could read what I wrote.

Art, dance, and music have been passions of mine that began before I could walk. As a teenager, I had the chance to send my woman sculpture to the Museum Of Modern Art (MOMA) in New York City for a contest. My teacher thought I had a decent chance at winning, but she also let me know that the piece could break in transit. I turned it down flat. "Are you sure?" she said.

Hiding

That piece helped save my life. I was sure I didn't want it to break. I also didn't want to win something and draw attention to myself. He could find me if I did that. He knew where we lived after Mom left him. It wasn't a secret. Fear isn't logical.

I wanted art school and a professional dancing career more than anything. I was trained in classical Russian ballet and had a deep passion for dance. I went to community college out of high school, rather than to a prestigious university. Big universities get recognition. My fear told me if I made it big in a field I loved, then Nightmare Man could find me and kill me. I wouldn't admit that to a soul, of course, because I was strong and 'fearless' was my middle name. I chose community college because they couldn't say no to me, couldn't hurt me with rejection of a dream. I denied my dreams and, in the process, allowed him to control my existence.

Turning down someone I loved in college wasn't a question of making myself happy. It was a decision to keep him safe. If I loved him, and I was happy, my ex-stepfather would come and kill him and end my happiness. It didn't register through my thick veil of fear that my love could've protected me. But I only knew I had to protect him. So, I walked away from him entirely. Part of me died the day I decided that. I locked the emotions away completely where they could be safe. But what did hiding cost me?

Later, after I had my associates degree in Liberal Arts, I moved several states away to continue my education. It wasn't until after I sent in my application that I realized I could be turned down. I shook when I thought about it but quickly shoved away that fear.

Medicine has always intrigued me. My mother was a

nurse, and my father had been a pre-med student once upon a time. Where medicine was concerned, my passion was more important than a fear I pretended didn't exist.

Some medical professionals will tell women not to have families if they want to be doctors. They're right in one way, that going to medical school (or any higher education, for that matter) while being a parent is a challenge. But applying this logic only to women is just hogwash. It should not matter if you're a man or a woman, a mother or a father. Balancing work life with a personal life is a challenge for everyone, no matter what job they have. Personally, I was fine with the idea of never having kids when I became a medical professional because it meant I could dive wholeheartedly into medicine, something that excited my mind and soul.

I embarked on pre-medicine as my focus. I got my EMT-B (Emergency Medical Technician-Basic) license, and volunteered at the Free Health Clinic where I could shadow doctors and triage patients. As graduation approached, I had decided I wanted to be a Doctor of Osteopathy, a D.O. The D.O. practice of treating the patient as a whole was intriguing, and I'd met an incredible mentor and teacher, Dr. M. He specialized in O.M.M., Osteopathic Manual Manipulation. He was at the Free Clinic and was an amazing teacher. He eventually left to help open a new Doctor of Osteopathy School. His passion was teaching and passing on the skills. I took the Medical College Admission Test and applied for D.O. school deliberately. I loved what they stood for and wanted that to be my career.

I was finally going to realize a dream. But when I got hurt lifting a patient into a dialysis chair, things

Hiding

changed drastically. I couldn't hold my own head up for more than two hours at a time. I was angry. I didn't do anything wrong while lifting, but I hadn't had enough sleep the night before. The human body isn't meant to run on two hours sleep. Burning the candle at both ends had a price. Mine was a muscle tear and a disc in my neck out of place for six months.

Constant pain brings fear up to the surface in a big way. Like any good survivor, I found a way to complete my bachelor's degrees and graduate. I did not apply to part two of medical school applications. Yoga and massage brought me back to the land of the healthy. I could have applied again when I healed, but I didn't. After all, I wanted to get a dual MBA and make medicine better. My fear told me that I shouldn't bother. Standing out is scary. The grieving for my deep desire to be a doctor took years.

As fate would have it, my road turned after the injury. I reexamined my life and asked myself why I'd been saying no to someone I loved. We got married, and had two beautiful children. I wouldn't change it for the world.

I spent decades of my life hiding so no one would see me. Staying in the shadows helped me stay alive. That's what I told myself. It felt comfortable. I'm not a fundamentally look-at-me person. I don't like it. I have physical reactions to doing anything that puts me in the spotlight. Actively avoiding positions of leadership, places where I could stand out or shine was a way of life. It was a knee jerk reaction to avoid such things in order to stay hidden. Choosing to become a part of something required some growth on my part. In recent years, I decided I would say yes to things that interested me in spite of the scared little girl hiding inside. Joining the parent volunteer group, Garden Club, and others were my first measures I took at stepping out of the shadows.

When I joined volunteer organizations, I was terrified. I didn't know if I could do the job the right way, be the best person for the job etc. Little things seemed big. What if I messed up? I felt a huge sense of responsibility to the school community and the organization to do a great job. I was ready for the challenge.

I dug in deep and used my creativity and time to help my children's school. What I gained from that experience was a true sense of family within that school community and being part of a collective "we". I belonged. My team and I were willing to step up to the plate and create new ideas, carve out new ideals and help the community thrive. The organization worked because we put the 'we' first, rather than one person's agenda. The time I spent on the board and volunteering there was rich and full of love. Seeing the smiles on the children and teacher's faces made it some of the most valuable volunteer work I've done to date.

Most things start with listening and are solved with love. Just those two things are integral to every single issue I've ever faced. There were years when I did not allow myself to listen to my own feelings. They felt dangerous and too scary for a long time.

Once I chose to open myself up and stretch myself as a human, it got easier. The first steps were the hardest. I loved the groups I joined and the lifelong friendships that were formed. The shaking grew less. I grew to be confident in my abilities and had faith in myself. While hiding felt comfortable, it also kept me very small. I didn't want to stay small anymore. Little by little, the hiding fell by the wayside. Sharing honestly and with love took its place.

As someone who hid her light for years, I can understand that it's scary to put yourself out there and be seen. Each time I have done so however, I have been better off for it. I realize that the world doesn't end just because my fear declared it.

Hiding a cancer doesn't stop that it exists. Left unchecked that cancer spreads, feeds and mutates good tissues into something foreign. Hiding did not stop the past from existing. It did not make me stronger in a long-term way. Hiding was a short-term fix for someone who was afraid they'd be killed. My life was different decades later. My insides, my emotions still festered. I hadn't dealt with the old pain.

Trusting isn't easy when someone breaks it so completely. Yet, within well placed trust are joy and love. It may not come natural or innately for me as it does for some. I am still able to trust. I am able to love. And, I always try to seek out the good in people. This is a choice I consciously make.

I also watched my dad deliberately choose not to hide anymore and to step out of the shadows. Dad climbed out of the darkness and into the light. Friends, family, and a lot of great memories were made during those times. Having watched him grow when I was young encouraged me even after he died.

I hated the word victim in all its pieces and parts for years. The truth is that things happened in my past. They were hard. They were traumatizing. They caused pain. I was more than those events. I was more than what happened, more than my fear. It was okay to admit I'd been scared.

I didn't shame myself for hiding. I didn't need it anymore to survive. I needed more. I needed to bloom above ground. I was gentle with myself and took the time I needed. Undoing old patterns takes time. I was in it for the long haul. I was building myself up again brick by brick.

Personal growth is like a rosebud growing and blooming. As the small green shell opens, the guard petals are seen. The bud grows and develops itself through nourishment. The large, full-grown rose is deep, full of layers and beauty.

I denied my dreams and, in the process, allowed him to control my existence.

But what did hiding cost me?

Anxiety: The Not-So-Shiny Bits

This will pass, I tell myself. I know it will. The achy worry in my chest doesn't stop instantly just because I know it will. It takes its own sweet time. Stupid anxiety.

Soul Fire

Some days there is anxiety. It shows up like a savage dog blocking your front door on your way to work in the morning. An unwanted, unwarranted visitor. There were several years where I lived with anxiety every single day. That was five years ago.

My trauma didn't happen yesterday. I wonder if my body is still addicted to that cortisol stress hormone. It took a while to detox my body when the craziness finally stopped. Those feelings of dread, constant worry, and heart racing became normal. I had to normalize peace in my body again. It takes almost nothing to activate that. Once your body experiences that feeling as normal, it takes something to shut off that fight or flight chain reaction.

My heart raced. My hands shook. I had nightmares. Dear lord, the nightmares! I was so tired of waking up having had yet another dream about someone trying to kill me. I suppose it's a tiny bit reassuring they didn't ever succeed. It didn't change the fact that I woke up with a feeling of dread, anger, and fear. Processing emotions sometimes sucks.

Cognitively, I get that the brain makes sense of things in our dreams. I understand that from a psychological point of view. The reality of the situation is still something I don't want constantly in my face.

Facing your demons is vital to living life fully. With that full life comes the whole freakin' gamut of emotions. Every. Single. One. Whether we like it or not.

There is a fallacy that human struggle is one battle. For those with temporary or even crippling anxiety, there are countless battles. For some, existing in the world is treacherous. My friend Lindsey said that "Existing in the world is treacherous but existing alone in solitude is so much worse. Tiny things become tremendous and suffocate you." Fighting the constant battles can be exhausting.

The key, I believe, is seeking and finding the healthy things that fill me up. Music can give voice to my emotions regardless of where I am on the rollercoaster. I have allowed music to give me purchase, validate my feelings, and fuel my Soul Fire that had grown dangerously low. The right song at the right time has been soothing for me countless times.

This will pass, I tell myself. I know it will. The achy worry in my chest doesn't stop instantly just because I know it will. It takes its own sweet time. Stupid anxiety.

A trauma counselor introduced me to the concept of trauma drive and the body's reaction when it stops and you begin to heal. Sometimes a lack of motivation to do anything at all comes as you heal from trauma. The body can slow down and rest because the mind knows it's finally safe. Actually safe. Those slow days are important. They are self-care even. There is a difference between taking the time you need to heal and just hiding from the anxiety.

When my dad died, I was crippled emotionally for a time. He was the foundation of my support system. He died suddenly after a surgery. My intuition told me he wouldn't survive. That didn't help the tsunami flood of emotions that swept me away in the aftermath. For four months, I was in a near paralyzed state. I did the bare minimum in my life to get to the next bedtime. Inevitably though, I couldn't sleep when the cloak of night came. Why? My mind would not shut off.

I allowed myself to watch movies my dad and I had watched together. I listened to music that we both loved. I remembered him. I cried. I felt bad for not sharing my "secret mommy" chocolate ice cream. I bought chocolate milkshakes from his favorite fast-food place and cried in the parking lot as I ate them. I remembered him buying four a week. One was for me. He always shared with me. I felt selfish and angry with myself for not doing more.

Eventually I remembered Dad lived with us for five years. We loved him, cared for him, and hopefully made the last five years full of love. He had grandchildren he saw every single day. He got hugged every single day. There were many years prior to him moving in that he didn't get hugged for months at a time. Knowing the beauty is there doesn't stop the pain from existing.

We hurt when we hurt. We cry when we cry. We grieve when we must grieve. The timeline feels arbitrary and deliberately hurtful at the same time. It's not on our time that these emotions come. Dyanne Joyner said in one R.A.W. (Rising Awakened Women) Inner Circle session, "We can't prevent them from ever existing. We can do our part not to slow down the process of healing, though."

She meant that by acknowledging the feelings fully, processing and letting go of the past when we can, healing takes place. On the contrary, if we stuff our feelings in a box, or numb the pain with food, alcohol, drugs or some electronic, then we delay the healing. It's our job to heal when we need to heal. As part of an exercise in R.A.W., I wondered, *if my best friend had gone through what I've been through, what would I tell her?* I'd tell her to take care of herself. Why is it so hard for us to give ourselves that same attention?

If my best friend came to me feeling incredibly anxious, I would listen to her. I would acknowledge her feelings and really listen. I would help her process out loud if she needed that. I'd buy her chocolate if she needed that. Guilt would not be part of that equation. Only love. I would love her.

So why, do I shame myself? Why do I feel like I must be perfect, and then hold it that it's okay for the rest of the world to be human? Am I an alien?

While looking inward, these things came up. I dealt with some of the hardest moments of my life. I said it was a choice to create happy. I stand by that statement. Simply saying that it was a choice left a big missing for me. It's also important to sit with your emotions sometimes, even if they aren't all sunshine and rainbows.

The concept of choice was affronting and assaulting to someone who has endured existing. She's someone who isn't afraid to go to the dark places because they're honest. They're not fake. Change requires going to those dark places and an altering of the truth as we know it. Those initial moments are a forced choosing of sorts. We force ourselves out of the comfy couch of despair or what we know to be true. We evolve our definitions from the truth we formed with our wounds to the truth that actually exists.

Sometimes, my inner wounded child wanted to punch my writer self in the face. What the heck do you mean, just choose? I asked myself this question repeatedly while writing and editing. I landed in a place that felt authentic. It finally hit me. Thankfully it wasn't literal.

As a child I was raised with the ideology that you make the choice, and the choice controls the chooser. Searching for the right words, I remembered this familial proverb, if you will. The concept was that I made a million tiny choices each day. When things snowballed in a nasty direction, I felt helpless. My grandmother reminded me lovingly that I made the choice, and the choice controlled the chooser. In other words, I was still responsible for me. I could change course. I could always change course. That concept gave me hope unlike anything else. It also confronted me about my own responsibility.

Pertaining to the concept of choice, I was reacting similarly to how some people react when others say your trauma makes you stronger. I was upset. Please know, if you react that way to some parts of what I say helped me endure, I understand. What we need in each moment is very different for each of us. Often what I needed wasn't what I wanted. It was very hard to be proactive when I spent so long reacting to the events that kept happening.

Years have been wasted letting inaction rule my life. I made the choice not to deal with fear and it ruled my life. One of the hardest things I ever did was make a phone call. I looked at my life and decided that I wouldn't let my worries control me or hold me hostage. I picked up the phone and spoke my truth. I'm not going to say who I called or what was said. The important part was that I did what I knew to be right. I knew I had to pick up the phone and dial. Once I finally did the thing that held me back, I was free.

It was sort of like a baby being free of their clothing or their diaper. I was raw and brand new. I still had to learn how to dismantle my old ways of thinking. Step by step I dealt with the old anxiety that haunted me daily.

What did I do though, to endure? What was the formula? I had to focus on the good in my life so I could get through the bad in each instance. When things were so much bigger than I could plan around, organize around, or pretend around, I dug in deeper. The consequences finally became bigger than the fear. All that was left was action. I may have flitted from one thing to the next. Yet, I deliberately chose relatively healthy things to get through the day. I began searching for the way out.

I put one foot in front of the other moment by moment as a teenager. I pretended I wasn't nearly as affected as I actually was. This helped me to get through each day. Years later, living through Aneurysm Alley, I pulled out my old standby, art and music. I added gardening and reaching out to friends into the mix. I had learned that stuffing it would not help.

Realistically, that huge wad of crazy train would never fit inside that tiny sleeping bag sausage wrapper of the past. My heartache spilled out everywhere. It was undeniable and unavoidable. Each moment became the focus when long term was ripped away entirely. I couldn't look ahead to the future. I had to deal strictly in what I was given that day. I was forced to be present. The strokes, his uncertain Navy career, my two young children were all so much together that I could not plan. I was a person who had a backup plan to my backup plan. Releasing all planning was a challenge.

When I got really sick with COVID, each breath became the focus. I listened to the birds chirping, my children laughing. I saw the beauty in the world so deeply. I listened to the *Hamilton* soundtrack and found the resilience there. I clung on with the strength I could muster.

It was hard to do that. But it was that much more important to feed that Soul Fire and give the good more credit. I was tempted by the dark side, so to speak. I have never stared so long and hard at the liquor cabinet as I did when I felt helpless to stop my husband from having strokes. I've never had a drinking problem, but I was very clear in that moment that it was far too dangerous to open a bottle. It would have been far easier to drown in the drink and numb the ever-constant pain.

I didn't want to feel the pain. I didn't want to be helpless. I wanted to fix the unfixable. I wanted my children to have a whole Daddy and a fun childhood. The hard times came whether I wanted them or not. I gave myself permission to be upset. I gave myself permission to disagree with my friends, loved ones, family and yes even the doctors. That permission gave me the resilience I needed for that set of circumstances.

The answer finally came to what was missing. I focused all my energy into the things that filled me up and brought joy to my heart. It wasn't out of some misguided need to deny the suck. I deliberately focused on the love and joy and scraps of happiness so I didn't drown.

When the tsunami shows up, it doesn't knock gently. Our reaction to it must have equal energy behind it in order to withstand that storm. That storm was so big and so all-encompassing that I would've drowned in an instant if I didn't put all my energy at the good in the world. I built my life raft so I could cling onto something and ride those gigantic waves. There was no denying the storm. I built myself a new vessel to come out on top.

Trying to ignore the storm by burying my head in the sand like an ostrich would have been catastrophic. When I re-read things I wrote like, "choose to be happy" and "insert joy here," my traumatized-self got upset. When my traumatized-self met the part of me that was trying to heal, I had to separate two superficially similar items. There is a difference between adding joy and goodness into your life and pretending that bad things aren't happening. Uncollapsing those two things gave me the space to manage my own anxiety. This gave me permission I didn't know I needed. My whole body relaxed. I settled into the space I had given myself. Freedom was a reality there. I had confused the ostrich method for my carefully crafted life raft.

You are allowed to be upset. It's part of being human. Sometimes things are upsetting. Make allowances for your own feelings. They will come whether we like them or not.

When polled, most people say that they enjoy the changing of the seasons. Usually, we all have a favorite. Some of us have strong negative feelings for one season. Does that make the season innately bad? No, of course not. Are we bad if we don't like to be cold in the winter? No.

We make allowances for our likes and dislikes as long as the thing we dislike is inanimate. You can't hold that thing called winter in your hands. You could in fact hold snow until your hands were numb. Snow itself does embody winter. Yet it is not the entirety of the thing called winter. Winter doesn't feel bad if we don't like it. So, who cares? We don't give it a second thought.

Why then, do we beat ourselves up when something upsets us? There are absolutely times when we need to deliberately look for and seek out the light and the positivity. If I didn't do that deliberate seeking, I'd likely be a drug addict, alcoholic, or dead. There's a time for that intentional crafting in our lives.

The flipside is also true. We must feel our unhappy, angry, sad, unsure thoughts in order to process them. It is in the processing that we allow them to exist. Dyanne says that people operate as if they need permission. She even gave us permission slips in R.A.W. We wrote out what we needed permission for. Usually, in our group it was some version of play. Right now, I give you permission to feel your feelings. Feel all of them, even if they aren't pretty.

Remind yourself that the anxiety, sadness, or grief will pass, even as you feel nearly swallowed by it. Give yourself permission to seek help from professionals if it really interferes with your life. The greatest strength I saw from my dad was when he sought therapy. He grew so much as a human. He gained coping skills for his OCD. Most importantly, he realized he was not broken. He was not crazy. He was a beautiful, amazing human. He learned that he had just as much right to this earth as anyone else. He learned that he deserved to belong. So please, if the harder emotions are preventing you from living life, reach out. You are worth it.

Emotions normally ebb and flow like the ocean. They may even feel like a hurricane at times. The coping skills I'm describing are for the short-lived, not dangerous levels of storm. They are not meant to replace a psychological professionals help or medical advice in any way.

Humans come with a wide array of emotions. Make allowance for all of them. It is in the allowing and the feeling of those emotions that those very waves can pass through and disperse.

Headaches make themselves known. If you have a headache and do nothing, will it go away? Maybe. However, it likely will stay with you and get worse.

Anxiety: The Not-So-Shiny Bits

Until you drink water to stop the dehydration, or take medicine, that headache persists. That old adage, "what you resist, persists" is true here as well. If you knew that you could just drink water and stop hurting, would you? Probably.

Translate that to our emotions. Allow yourself to process all emotions. If you resist dealing with the grief, it will remain there, under the surface. It will inevitably randomly explode all over your friends and family. Anger, anxiety, sadness, these are all the same. Ignoring them will not make them go away. Processing them through writing, talking with someone you trust, or even doing something creative helps. If you knew right now, today, that processing the emotions worked, would you give yourself permission?

My husband had stroke after stroke over a two-year period. The first three we didn't even notice. The fourth was the brick wall that hit us all square in the face. Processing the emotions that came with that uncertainty took something.

It required patience I didn't have. I had to go find the patience. Sometimes, chocolate ice cream gave me patience. Calling a friend to vent worked far better. If I still had a head full after that call, I called someone else. I talked with Dad. I talked to anyone who would listen. My mind ran on repeat for a long time. In the thick of it, reaching out and feeling what was demanding to be felt was required.

I didn't like it. I was mad as hell about it. It took all I had to marry and fully trust someone with all of me. It took even more to walk away from my career and follow him as the military spouse. Raising my children while he was at sea was the obvious choice to me. It also made me, the strong independent woman, feel very vulnerable. So, imagine all that independence with no career and a Navy man who'd had multiple strokes. I was mad as a hatter. That was my worst nightmare.

I had to allow myself to feel that anger. My children didn't need to feel that anger. I did. So, I talked until I was empty with friends during naptimes and after bedtimes. I made fairy gardens during the day with them to create space for them to be children. They needed to just be children. It was far more important that I didn't damage them with my emotions than anything else. I did the best I could. When I made mistakes, I owned up to them.

I learned a lot about the resilience that humans are capable of during that time. I learned that my husband really preferred the "ignore it until it goes away" method. He learned that he had to face the strokes in order to recover and heal physically and emotionally.

We are stubborn. Two-by-four therapy sometimes is required in times like these. I don't mean literally hitting someone over the head. It's metaphorical. Two-by-four therapy is giving someone the truth when they really need it. It's often the tough conversation that most would prefer to skip or pretend around.

For my husband, John, it was a conversation about his physical and occupational therapy. I let as much time go by as I could. I let him process on his own, think, be, play video games. He still wasn't working to heal. So, we had the talk. No, not that talk. We stood in the kitchen, and I asked him a serious question.

"Do you want to heal?" I asked, looking him square in the eye.

He shifted a bit on the other side of the kitchen island. "Of course I do." He replied barely meeting my gaze.

Anxiety: The Not-So-Shiny Bits

"You're going to have to work for it then. You're on a timeline whether you like it or not. The first six months after a stroke are the most important to work the physical and occupational therapies. The most healing takes place during that first six months. If you want to walk a straight line again, or to stop being dizzy, you're going to have to work for it."

He sighed. He realized that avoidance was no longer an option. He started his mandated month of leave by proving he could still do something. He built solid red oak bookshelves. They ran the length of the room above the garage. He topped off that month with as much video game time as he could muster. He also hid. He hid from the reality. He hid from the "s" word. He hid from that hard truth that he had a stroke at thirty-eight years old. He hid from the fact that his dad's stroke, a few years prior, gave him near total apraxia and aphasia.

John's brilliant, amazing father could no longer talk. He couldn't tell the difference between a toothbrush and a razor. The thought of not being able to provide for his own family traumatized my husband to the point of paralyzing him with fear. John wasn't ready for his life to be over.

My two-by-four therapy conversation was exactly what he personally needed in that moment. He had to be snapped out of his emotions for long enough to make a choice, rather than just react. He chose therapy. He chose that straight line. It pissed him off. He chose to practice walking the line anyway.

He grumbled. He griped and complained. He still followed the crack on the back porch floorboards and held his arms out straight. He did the exercises the PT and OT gave him religiously. He judged himself harshly. He also put in the work. That very work he put in changed his life completely. I let him complain. I tried to listen. I sent him to my dad too, who had been there with his own strokes. I'm sure Dad listened too.

The bottom line is that he did the work. He felt how he felt. He did what he did. They weren't the same in that case. He felt stupid and childish and humiliated and humbled walking a line like a drunk on the side of the road. He felt fear that the Navy would kick him out just a few years shy of retirement with nothing. He was terrified that he couldn't put food on the table or a roof over our heads. He was the sole provider and didn't know if he could do that right.

He did every exercise as if his life depended on it. I had painstakingly explained that it would not likely get any better unless he trained his brain to create new pathways. He did the work. John needed to allow for his feelings, all of them. He didn't want to. He really didn't want to face the reality that he'd had a stroke, let alone four of them, by that point. He steeled his resolve anyway and set up and followed an exercise schedule. He did his best to let go of the doubt and self-judgement. He let it spill out if it bubbled out. **And**, he did the work.

Because of that hard work he did, he was able to drive a car again. The visual and auditory stimulation were far too much for him to take in the beginning. The first time I drove him onto the highway, he nearly puked on the onramp. He saw the cars going both ways on the highway ahead, felt the car steering to the right, and heard the radio and me talking all at once. It was too much.

I paused at his "Oh geez!" and saw him covering his eyes with his hands. I asked him what happened. He

Anxiety: The Not-So-Shiny Bits

couldn't talk. I drove in silence. I'm not usually silent. This was painful. It was scary for me too. Imagine what he must've been feeling!

John described what happened as we rounded that onramp onto the freeway. We quickly realized that the noises in the house were overstimulating him too. We worked together as a family to cope, practice, and help John heal over the two years in what I now call Aneurysm Alley.

We all had big feelings, even the children. They didn't understand at two and three what was happening or why Daddy was upset. We tried, in bite size toddler chunks to give them answers. We didn't have all the answers.

Those two years were filled with anxiety, anger, and grief. They also held tender love, babies growing up, and healing. Each member of the family had to feel every emotion in order to function. It was all so big that we could not let anything build up in denial. That would've been ineffective and frankly dangerous.

The most dangerous issue we had in the beginning was the stove. John loved to cook. He was great at it. He couldn't remember to turn the stove or the oven off anymore. That small thing gets dangerous really fast with two small children and their grandfather in a wheelchair in the same house.

Anger boiled over like water on the stove if I talked about the oven. He lashed out at me for two years. I tried not saying anything and turning it off myself. I tried saying I was turning it off as I did it. I tried doing nothing and waiting to see if he remembered on his own. He didn't. More than half of the time John touched the stove or oven, he left it on. Anytime I said or did anything, he was angry.

Soul Fire

I was very tired of being the bad guy for protecting the house after two years of this merry-go-round. One day, the answer hit me. I'd been staring it in the face the whole time. The lightbulb went on. I asked him tentatively one day, if he thought turning the light on under the microwave would help him remember to turn off the stove.

"We never turn that light on," he said quizzically.

"Exactly," I said. "That's why it could help. It's right in front of our faces above the stove. We will see it and think it's strange. Maybe it's the key to remembering to turn off the stove!"

Sure enough, that did the trick. Just like that, the danger passed. While we ignored it, evaded it, and pretended it away, it persisted. We both were finally willing to look at the issue. We looked at the problem and saw a possible solution. It worked. The light reminded us to look at the knobs and ensure that they were off.

John's strokes were in the cerebellum of the brain where voluntary movements such as walking and speech are held. He could still function for the most part. Why then, was the stove the thing that he forgot? I have no clue. The brain is a fascinating, frustrating mystery.

What I do know is that the solution required teamwork and a willingness. We both had to accept that this thing we didn't want existed. We accepted our feelings about it, fear and all. Then, we looked for an answer. Several years down the line, that stove issue is a distant memory. Our everyday lives are no longer run by it. What a miracle that is!

There were two years I couldn't leave my husband at home alone with the children. His children! It was hard. It was scary. It was maddening. Trying to fix it on my own felt like hitting my head against a brick wall. From one stubborn human to another, that man was stubborn! He had to sort through his feelings about it. I had to sort through mine. We each had to realize that our feelings about the situation did not take away our love for each other.

The strokes did not render him useless. The strokes by themselves had no meaning. There was a slew of things to deal with after the strokes. When he later had surgery to repair the aneurysm they found, there were even more things to handle. We took them on like it was our job. We finally took that same stance with the stove and accepted that it existed. We felt our feelings. We talked, yelled, cried, and reasoned. After that, we could finally let go of all the added emotions like water. That's what it took.

Going through life does not have a one size fits all "How To" manual. We want it to. We wish it did. It doesn't. Life throws us curve balls. During those years, I wondered, was the Universe bored? It had to shake things up, just for fun. The truth is we learned a lot from that time. We grew as individuals, and later as a couple. We grew as parents, too.

The hard times remind us how to appreciate the sweet times. Do we have to go through hard times? I think we do, even though it's uncomfortable. Sometimes we also make things much harder than they have to be by avoiding the discomfort.

Give yourself permission to feel the full gamut of emotions. Process. Take time for yourself. Try to look at what's actually happening or happened rather than worry about what **might** happen. It's not easy. It is worth it.

If the tsunami comes barreling down on you, find the wood and sails to make your own life raft. When the seas are calmer, allow for the time it will take to wrap your head and heart around the entirety of what happened. Process. It takes exactly as long as it takes.

We take our experiences and create what we will from them. We do that ourselves. Trauma didn't do that by itself. The saying that trauma makes you stronger really upsets some people. Each person gets triggered by completely different things. For example, that statement doesn't upset me nearly as much as denying the storm existed in the first place. I denied the depth and breadth of my own storm for years. That survival coping mechanism did not have to overshadow my life. I began to choose life over the very old fear. Building new patterns of thought and action was not comfortable. It did get easier with repetition and time.

Anxiety and fear are bedfellows. They often are rooted within each other. Some say that they are two words for the same thing. Unravelling each of them requires slightly different vantage points. Anxiety can be the physical manifestations of the emotions like fear. I have felt paralyzed by fear and anxiety. Anxiety is a symptom, not the emotion itself.

I combat anxiety with several different things. Although some parts of my past told me that it wasn't safe, I find someone I trust to share what's going on. Telling my friend how I'm feeling helps me to understand what's all wadded up inside. I pull on the tangled ball of yarn and inspect it. Someone else may do this through journaling. In the instances when things are really amped up, I pull out all the stops. Journaling, talking, listening to music, cleaning, exercising, painting, and walking outside are all possibilities that help. I may flit from one to the next like a very hungry mosquito. I may even feel stupid for trying the cliché things. I do them anyway because I know they work for me.

The actual thing I do in each instance does not matter. What matters is that I give myself the space, love, and acknowledgement to process everything I feel in a healthy way. What matters is that I do not stay stuck in any one thing like anxiety. I know that anxiety will not stay as strong as it is in one moment. I trust myself. I trust that if I put in the work, like my husband did with his stroke recovery, it will pay off.

Doing the work helps me move through the thing. On the other side of that uncomfortable thing I wish didn't exist is more knowledge and more trust. I trust myself more. I forgive myself more. I love myself more. Faith and trust in myself helps me endure the moments that are harder. When I can't see, taste, or touch peace of mind; I know it will come.

We don't know ourselves very well because we don't want to be uncomfortable. We don't want to feel bad, ever. We forfeit peace of mind through avoidance of feelings. We will do anything to avoid the bad stuff in our instant gratification world. In doing that, we give up the ability to grow, change and trust ourselves. We give up loving who we are. We give up our whole lives. Avoidance is not worth that much to me. That's too high a price. Anxiety can sometimes be a piece of the whole. As we heal, the experience lessens over time. We grow to have more faith in ourselves and in the healing process. It takes practice to get to that point. When I practiced tying my shoes, I got better at that too.

Soul Fire

 *When the tsunami shows up, it doesn't knock gently. Our reaction to it must have equal energy behind it in order to withstand that storm.*

Fear Lies To You

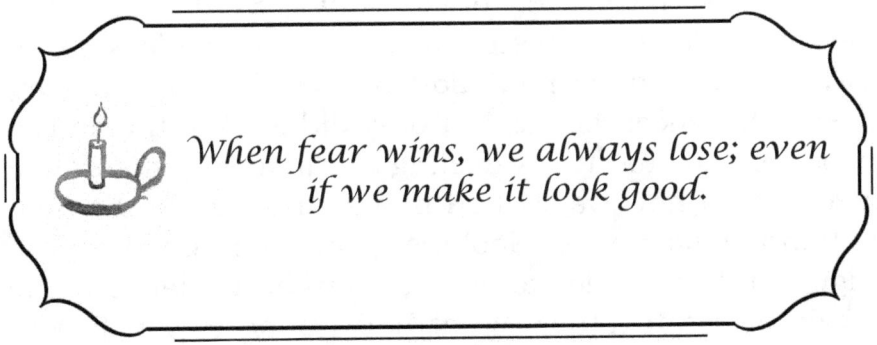

When fear wins, we always lose; even if we make it look good.

Fear can be crippling, much like anxiety. Simply put, fear is your body's way of telling you that something could be dangerous or cause unwanted results. Perceived danger comes up in most definitions of the word fear. What if the perception is skewed? What if the body reacts to something that was bad one time under many other situations for a long after the initial event? Fear then becomes a recurring tsunami without any water. The body feels that terror or dread of the impending storm. The storm doesn't come, however. Our body created it to avoid a **possible** threat.

How then, does one stop the fear cycle? I first had to allow the fear in. I had to accept that I had been afraid. That first wave of terror when I was a teenager was something I did not allow myself to really feel. In order to heal, I realized that I first had to allow my feelings to exist. This required support, of course. The twenty-five-year-old tsunami was huge whether I pretended it away or not. I had to walk through the door.

That day in the front room as my father was dying, I decided to stop the cycle of fear. It was **my** turn to grow and be the elder. I systematically made choices to be brave where I once had hidden myself...to be honest, where I had been silent. Not only did I make the choice to be honest about my feelings, but it felt imperative that I find a new way. I had no idea how to do the task at hand. I started by looking at what happened, the original trauma. I looked at how my brain had put the puzzle pieces together. What had I done to cope? Why did I do it? What would I do instead in order to change?

The desire to be more than I used to be for my children's sake far outweighed the old fear. Fear would no longer win, but that didn't mean it just went away. When given the choice to retreat inside or to reach out,

Fear Lies To You

I chose to reach out. My coping skill had been to hide. Yet, I saw that reaching out helped separate the emotion of fear from the thing itself. It actually helped. Reaching out wasn't all hogwash! Each act of bravery would steel my resolve. One day I looked up the definition of bravery and what I found made me chuckle. And old fashioned use of the word was "fine clothes." (Merriam-Webster, s.v. "Bravery") I contemplated bravery as if it was something I could put on and take off again. Sometimes when I did what had to be done, I felt like I donned my Sunday bravery, rather than owned it.

I started by saying yes when my fear would irrationally tell me to say no. One by one, I joined a parent volunteer organization, my local garden club, and other groups to be more than I was yesterday. I joined because I had interests in my children's schools, in gardening, the church I grew up in, and in education. I joined to give back to my community. I was also terrified each time I said "yes". I did it despite that fear. Quickly the people welcomed me into the communities. The shaking faded. I felt at home there. It became normal to talk to people. Growing out of my shell took something.

Each group I was a part of came with the possibility of my name being put in print in newspapers. Each time someone could **see** me, it meant that my ex-stepfather, who threatened to kill me, could find me. The fear was still winning until I deliberately chose 'yes' in the face of this very old fear. Each step I took in the uncomfortable unknown gave me a bit of freedom and self-expression.

Then the global pandemic hit in March of 2020.

Note: Merriam-Webster, s.v. "Bravery," accessed February 28, 2023, https://www.merriam-webster.com/dictionary/bravery

Soul Fire

What does a global pandemic feel like to a survivor? I can only speak for me. When 9/11 happened, I was living in New York state. It finally felt like I could express the feelings I had safely, and that other people could understand. We, as Americans, all felt something when the Twin Towers went down. For me, the pandemic felt very similar. It was a forced 'hiding' that I'd worked so very hard to escape from! I was forced into a box for very real, very safe reasons. For three years prior to the pandemic, I had begun saying yes to things that made me nervous. By the time March of 2020 came, I had worked quite hard at coming out of my shell.

How do you not move backwards when faced with that reality? I chose my circle of people deliberately and safely. Reaching out to people and taking a long hard look at what was right in front of me became priorities.

You would think with the pandemic that it couldn't get worse, right? Wrong. My mother was diagnosed with metastatic lung and brain cancer the same week we went into lockdown. Global pandemic and metastatic cancer in one week. In my mind, I'd come too far to lose emotional ground. I would not retreat into a hidey-hole. Mom and I chose instead to believe in miracles in every moment throughout her cancer journey. We deliberately chose love rather than fear.

During her radiation, Mom and I met a lovely man around my mother's age. His brown eyes smiled behind the mask on his face. He floated over to us. The meeting was in stark contrast to the fear of COVID. It stood in contrast to the fear of cancer, and even to the fear of death. He was very quickly nicknamed Mr. Godsend. Every day since, I've gotten a text or a call.

Fear Lies To You

The tidbits of joy and meaningful connection always offer something I need to hear.

"Work towards your life's purpose each and every day," Mr. Godsend told me one day. Mom must've said some very kind things about me that day while I was volunteering at my children's school. He became family that next day. We learned all about his collage art, the civil rights history he was steeped in, and the blessing on earth he was to everyone he met.

He still calls me to explain a collage or photograph he'd sent. It's hard for me to believe even now that we've only known each other a short time. Some days, he echoes the sentiments of my father so completely, that it takes my breath away.

"With each step you take in the direction of your dreams, you honor yourself and your family," Mr. Godsend says. Almost nothing is worth hiding forever for and there's always a better way than slinking through each day.

I believe that Mr. Godsend listens when the Universe, God, and people speak. He listens, even and especially, when they do not speak. I ask myself: *if you're honest, are you working towards your life's purpose each day? Or are you listening to the fear's lies?*

I've often compromised what I want for the greater good. I told myself that it was for the family. I told myself a lot of things over the years. The truth is that it also allowed me to feel 'safe' when I did not step into the light of my life's purpose. When fear wins, we always lose; even if we make it look good.

Fear can make even the silliest of things seem rational. A dear friend has given me several books written by successful women who have found their fire. I was afraid of change and therefore had not allowed myself to read them. How dare I? What kind of example am I to my children if I'm not willing to honestly be myself every day, and striving to be a better person? Being afraid of change should not hold me back. I am well aware that it's easy to type those words and much harder to take the actual steps. I read the books. Each time I've stepped out on a limb, it's paid off.

One of the biggest limbs I ever stepped out on was when I said 'yes' to a relationship with the man who eventually became my husband. This was back when fear was behind many of my choices. Fear was underlying most of my choices. I was in college at the local university studying biology, exercise science, and was also a pre-medicine student. Pre-med, as they say, was not a degree at that particular university. Finding a backup plan to my backup plan was a survivor's skill I had honed with care. A bachelor's degree in biology is not incredibly useful in the real world without a teaching certificate, but at the time I didn't want to teach. My family and friends were teachers and I saw how hard they worked and the politics involved. Exercise science was my back up plan and core to who I was as a dancer. I firmly believed that health and wellness should be at the core of medicine.

The Diner became home for me as a workplace just after Hurricane Isabel wreaked havoc on the east coast of the United States in October of 2003. My husband is among those I met while working at the Diner as a server. I was in college at the university and dating someone else at the time. The servers each had their regulars. Sometimes that meant that folks waited thirty minutes to an hour for a table with their preferred server. Why would anyone wait an hour for breakfast? People waited outside the shiny metal 1950s style diner for a small taste, literally and figuratively, of home. Some waited because they loved the food. Some loved the coffee. Most people that came back time and again did so because they knew what to expect when they came. It was familiar. They knew they'd be greeted by someone at the hostess desk warmly. They knew that once they got to their table, the staff would be attentive and get them what they wanted. If they were famous, they knew if they came to the Diner, they'd be treated as a regular human regardless of their football scores or the latest song they'd produced. The military people I knew at least came to the Diner because the food was great. John, a single lieutenant at the time, came there because it was geographically between his work on the military base and his townhome. Sometimes he'd be out walking and stopped there for dinner on the way home. He had a usual server, Natalie.

One day in particular, Natalie was working as a manager and asked me to take care of "T-bone" for her. He was termed "T-bone" by the staff because he came in and ordered T-bone steak and eggs every time with water. I immediately learned two things about T-bone. First, bring two thirty-two ounce glasses of water without ice immediately. He would drink the first glass faster than you can blink. One of the worst things you can do as a server is to let your guests' drinks run dry. Secondly, I noticed he came in alone but always with a book.

Men can be scary sometimes when it was a man who originally made you a victim. I choke on these words, even writing them. First of all, it's not in my nature to expose the truth that men scare me. Secondly, the words "I am not a victim" have left my lips several million times in this lifetime. It is the truth though. In the past, men scared me. All men. I had a visceral reaction to just looking at them and could scarcely look them in the eye. I was not willing to live in that place of fear forever though.

I took care of T-bone whenever he came in. He started asking for me regularly on the weekends. I always gave him the attention and care required but no more. I didn't deliberately chat. He had broad shoulders and a large muscular frame. The survivor in me had many things to say about being overpowered by such a frame. The survivor in me did not like the thought of being put into that position ever by anyone.

Yet, he was kind and respectful. His blue eyes didn't look menacing at all. I reminded my survivor self that he was not my triggers. He didn't have to be bad just because one bad person had done bad things. One particular morning I allowed myself to be curious and to see what was actually there; I looked at his book. He was reading *Harry Potter And The Prisoner Of Azkaban* in hard cover. Wow. That stopped me in my tracks. It did not support my prejudices at all. I allowed them to slip away. I allowed myself to see the human who was actually at my table that morning. Anyone reading Harry Potter must have a sense of humor, I told myself.

The ice wall chipped away, and a courteous friendship evolved. I wasn't looking for love at that time. Several years and four college degrees between us later, we did date and eventually marry. That future could have slipped away entirely if I had not allowed myself to see the Harry Potter book. It would have been so much easier to hide in my prejudices and my fear. Yet, the life we've lived since those Diner days has been incredible. We've lived on both coasts, explored life, and created two beautiful bright children together.

Fear Lies To You

Following your heart sometimes requires growing new capacities that may at first be scary. When it comes to fear, practicing doing what you love makes it easier. The more you do that new thing you feel called to do, the less new it will seem. The more you go out of your comfort zone, the more you stretch your own perceived boundaries. Sometimes we do things we love even with fear in the background. The fear may not go away entirely. We get to tell it when to sit down and be quiet. Love outweighs fear if we let it. It's easier to tell fear to sit down if we are following our life's purpose and fueling our Soul Fire.

It will get easier to speak in public with practice. It will be easier to be 'seen' by people with practice. I am certain it's important to be our best selves each and every day. If I deny my gifts, or my purpose in life, then I'm wasting time. I wasted too much time allowing fear to win. I'm done wasting time for the sake of fear or hiding.

In the past, I have apologized too much. I was afraid people wouldn't like me. A friend once said, "Sarah, you'd apologize if the sky was blue whether it was your fault or not." Since she was both an honest person and incredibly intelligent, my lizard brain said, "she's right." The lizard brain is responsible for our fight or flight decisions and autonomic responses. I can tell you that my lizard brain has had quite a workout in this lifetime.

Breaking the cycle of fear here takes something. I understand that it's not an easy habit to break. Slowly over years, I've trained myself to avoid apologizing when it's not my fault. The fear still rises in my gut sometimes. I still want people to like me whether I should want them to or not. I'm trying to evolve, piece by piece, moment by moment.

2020 was a year of evolution for the world, microbes, politics, science, and naturally, a lot of us. Personally speaking, I'm a social creature. It makes me happy to help people. If I am being useful, contributing to society, big or small, then it brings me joy. That year, we were all forced to make our circles smaller. The people I let into my circles were more authentic and meaningful. There was a big hole where the rest of my circle once stood.

In March of 2020 I focused on my inner value, my inner evolution. Quickly that focus shifted to my mother's health and her fight against lung cancer. By June she was gone. I spent all of July sick in bed with COVID, and was alive to bury my parents on August 22nd. Who knew I'd be so unbelievably grateful to be above ground?

I enjoy life. Art, dance, music, friends, and love fill me with joy and hope. I'm an optimist in spite of every experience I've been near, around, or come out the other side of. Each experience is a lesson and I long to be taught. I was that child who loved to learn. I still am. I guess I got that from my mother. How odd that I didn't know it until she was dying?

For decades I've said 'every day is a gift' and meant it. That's no different now. It's deeper, more powerful, and so much more meaningful. Finally, the fear in me is smaller than the deep knowing that I must share these experiences. Someone out there needs to know they're not alone. Someone needs to know that how they're feeling isn't wrong, or bad. I know that I am no longer willing to allow the old knowing, the old ways, and the old fear to cloud my todays and steal my tomorrows. I allowed that in the past. I get to choose now and every day I'm given here on this earth.

Fear Lies To You

Sometimes God's two-by-four therapy is the way that I have to learn the lesson. Some of us, like me, have to get beat over the head with the same idea for decades before we learn the lesson.

Life gives us opportunities to get better. Sometimes it feels like I'm training for the Olympics. Sometimes I need a rest in between training. Other times, pushing through full steam ahead is required.

All those years ago, I knew a day would come when the fear would become smaller than what I was called to do with my life. I could've been an artist. I could've been a dancer. I could've been a doctor. However, I didn't pursue those things. When I stepped past the fear, I reexamined all the lives I was too afraid to choose and began to grieve. It was a part of the grieving process for a hundred lives I was too scared to choose.

Fear lies to you. Fear and OCD go hand in hand. With OCD, something bad happens or almost happens, and you develop a fear. Maybe it doesn't actually happen, but you're afraid that it will. So, you do things to combat that foreign enemy, fear. If you're afraid you'll be late to work, then you repeatedly check your alarm clock. If you're afraid of a house fire, you may repeatedly check your stove. The list goes on and on. The lie inside of that scenario is that checking the alarm clock will prevent you from being late. But, if you hit snooze fifty times, then you'll be late regardless.

People I love dearly lived with OCD their whole lives. It can be very debilitating and life-altering. If you ask someone with OCD, they will likely admit that the house isn't likely to catch on fire, but they are still gripped by the negative possibilities and the fear. I had my own brand of afflictions with fear.

Fear lied to me and told me that if I didn't tell anyone that I was hiding in all the little ways, then I wasn't really a victim. Somehow, not verbalizing what actually happened made it easier to pretend. If I pretended that I didn't really want to dance or to do art anyway, then it was ok for part of me to be hidden away.

When I was going through the worst things in my life, no one knew. If I didn't tell anyone how dangerous he was, then they would be safe. The truth is, if someone wants to kill you, they will. It rarely makes good sound logical sense. I left a trail of breadcrumbs large enough to be seen from space. Murder is still senseless and horrific like cancer. If he wanted to kill me, then he would have. My wits would not have necessarily stopped him.

It's worth mentioning here that I'm proud of leaving those breadcrumbs and for surviving. It was not easy. That pride is also the path to stroking the ego of the survivor. We tell ourselves that we did it. We made it. We survived this horrible thing. And that, like checking the alarm clock for a person with OCD, also feeds the thought process that we affected that change and prevented more horrible things from happening. That same pride keeps us alone and reluctant to trust anyone or allow others to help us. It is therefore the means to our survival and our undoing.

The goal now is to stop the fear cycle and be able to evolve beyond the history of your life. Acknowledging what I went through was absolutely required for me to begin healing. I had to be with the pain and all the emotions therein in order to let them go. I had to realize that I am more than the things that have happened to me.

Each person, regardless of their experiences, has their own perceptions. I can only speak about my own and pray that it gives others the courage to do the work of their lives.

Someone kind listened to my full story when I was ready to share. I hadn't told the story yet. I was ashamed, had survivors' guilt, and a lot of fear because of an abusive man that had married my mother under false pretenses. Telling them the story that I'd held onto in fear, the truth freed my soul. Telling them everything without publicizing it gave me the ability to breathe deeply that day and in the days since. I'm forever grateful.

The honest truth is that since the original trauma, I have, in part, let fear win and be prioritized in my life. Over five years, I worked hard at systematically dismantling the fear that I allowed to bind me. I will not let fear win.

These things are not my sole motivator. I am moved by the two brilliant, loving humans that I have the pleasure of raising. They deserve a role model that reaches for the stars. They deserve a mom who is brave enough to speak up when something is wrong, and someone who's moving towards their life's purpose. I cannot be that while in hiding to protect myself or them. I cannot simultaneously hide and thrive. I cannot both live and allow fear to win.

Some days it seems like the whole world is against me. I just want to scream that it's not fair. I'm old enough to know that if I decide that is the absolute truth then I defeat myself at the starting point.

I have developed a safety threshold of about five or six. This means that I don't panic at the first thing that goes wrong. I can keep a level head and move through whatever's going on until five or six things happen concurrently. When that threshold gets breached, it's

Soul Fire

not pretty. One such cluster happened and enlightened me further.

The main battery needed to be replaced on the alarm system. The back door was busted, and the handle kept falling off. Then the van's battery died for some unknown reason. I had just gardened and was in pain afterwards. Then, my daughter's glasses went missing. A few days later the twelve-year-old dishwasher had a control lock light that didn't want to shut off. Then the washer and dryer both started acting up like icing on the nasty cake. The conglomerate resulted in me being very cranky and unhappy for a bit. The washer and dryer stopped me in my tracks. It was over the top, too many 'coincidences' to ignore. For a brief moment I wanted to throw my hands in the air and scream at the Universe. "Are you not entertained?!" I laughed at the absurdity and took it in that those moments had something for me to learn.

Some things break down from time to time. Occasionally, more than one thing happens at once. Sometimes six things happen all at one time. When I vented about the situation, my mentor said that I was "good at connecting the dots." It woke me up very suddenly to the fear cycle. It can be really easy to fall into when we're focused on the day to day.

One of my most favorite sayings that Dad said repeatedly was that there was never enough time with those we loved. When my mentor said that about the dots, it clicked that there's never enough placating the fear either if we let it take over.

The old Cherokee legend about the two wolves is a great story to live by. In the legend, the grandfather explains that we all have two wolves inside us. One is fear, anger, hatred, and darkness. The other wolf is light and love and grace and kindness. The grandson asks him which wolf wins? The grandfather replies, "the one you feed."

In this case, the wolf we feed is either fear or love, just surviving life or living it. Fear and love are both natural, normal parts of our lives. When multiple things broke down at the same time, I fed the fear for a brief moment. We all do from time to time. I realized that fear and love are the same in some ways. There is never enough time with those we love. Nothing you do to placate the fear will actually make it go away. These two things are both true.

Conversely, love and those we grieve for after they're gone are worth that pain and our love. Fear exists to keep us safe. And there are times when we allow that fear to run rampant like a child on a junk food eating spree. There are times when we long to hide away our hearts to protect ourselves from pain. Too much of that kind of safety net can become our undoing. The yin and yang of life is meant to be in balance. When it isn't in balance, we know it, even if we don't know what it is yet.

To live, is to acknowledge fear, but to not let it rule you, to be courageous and move purposefully towards your light. Each of us has at least one thing that stirs our souls. I believe each of us is called to a higher purpose than ourselves. We may achieve that goal any number of ways and may choose any number of careers. If we are to be alive, not just survive, then we must listen to our 'gut instincts', angel guides, whatever you call it and move with purpose.

When we listen to that inner power, to the light inside us, we are at peace in our skin. When we hide from it, distract from it, or do something opposed to it, we are wrestling with ourselves, our souls, and what we know to be true every second of every day. When we don't take care of ourselves, we get sick. It may be lack of sleep, pushing too hard to be the perfect executor of your mother's will, or just denying your life's purpose. Each of these things takes us away from the light, regardless of our backgrounds.

There is never a good time to give in to darkness. Macbeth was morose when he said:

> Tomorrow, and tomorrow, and tomorrow,
> Creeps in this petty pace from day to day,
> To the last syllable of recorded time;
> And all our yesterdays have lighted fools
> The way to dusty death. Out, out, brief candle!
> Life's but a walking shadow, a poor player,
> That struts and frets his hour upon the stage,
> And then is heard no more. It is a tale
> Told by an idiot, full of sound and fury,
> Signifying nothing.
>   William Shakespeare

However, William Shakespeare was speaking to the 'poor player', those who did not fully live life. The truth is that every life isn't a 'walking shadow'. One truth that I believe he was getting to is that when you don't live your truth, live deeply, you're not really alive. You're a shadow of a life if you let fear win.

As humans, we are all more alike than we are different. We should love each other more than fear each other. Mahatma Gandhi, The Dalai Lama, Buddha, they have that right! Love is the answer, just like the flower children of the 1960s said.

Fear is not an enemy any more than grief. They're both part of being human no matter what we wish were true. The key is to acknowledge the fear or grief and choose for myself. Fear may always try to go to lunch with me, but I don't have to allow it to have a seat. I could say "thank you for trying to protect me, Fear. I'm not interested today." I am the architect of my own life. I get to say.

I've kept a journal since I got my first one at eleven years old. Some people write every day. Some write when important things happen to them or around them. I usually write to make sense of my jumbled thoughts, the monkey brain as Buddhists call it. If I've spun my wheels one too many times, I write to be able to empty out emotionally.

During the worldwide COVID pandemic, 9/11 felt bigger and much less than nineteen years ago. Mr. Godsend suggested I write down everything I experienced that day. "It's part of your direct history," he said.

"Yes sir," I replied. So, I began writing. Suddenly, it hit me. In those nineteen years, I had filled four journals and one book of my poetry. Not one has an entry on September 11th.

When I asked myself why, the reply came from a deep place, "Because, when the really scary things happen, you stuff them away and do anything **but** share them." That's my body's automatic response rooted in fear and self-preservation. On September 11, 2001 my body viscerally went back in time to the prior traumatic events when I felt unsafe. Inside, I felt like the next plane could hit us where we were. Maybe that is the ego talking. It was my truth of that day.

When I first went to write down what happened when I was a teenager, the journals were remarkably empty. I knew that my stepfather could read everything I wrote and would destroy it or destroy me if I wrote the truth about him down. I wrote poetry instead. It felt safer. I had to protect myself in other ways, like never being alone with him. My stepfather's anger was palpable in moments like when he was smashing dishes against the wall.

He was a systematic abusive personality. Every single thing he did made it abundantly clear that he hated me. So, when he threatened to kill me, it wasn't really a surprise. Everything he did, it seemed to me, was rooted in fear. I was supposed to be afraid of him.

The time living with my stepfather forever changed me, even if it took me years to admit. I allowed it to change me. He was capable of immense evil, and likely capable of murder. He gloated on more than one occasion he'd been let go by police for cocaine possession. People at the business he owned feared him, but I didn't know why until it was too late.

Around the same time, my dad took a programming job in Georgia to learn COBOL, a new computer programming language. That put him states away from me. The consolation prize was a pager. My stepfather's answer to that was to cut off the house phone. He did everything in his power to cut me off from anyone who knew me. He wanted me to stop going to my school and my dance studio. I knew that I'd be dead, literally, if that happened. So, I told my mother I'd move to Georgia if she made me do it. My instincts knew he was full of hatred and anger long before he threatened to kill me. His choices all supported that gut instinct, from drugs to his anger and fervent efforts to isolate my mother and me. If he could have loved himself, would things be different?

Choosing to survive and feed the light was the only option for me as a teenager. I had one moment of being so far in the dark, I did not acknowledge even to myself how much he scared me. If my mother was going the paranoid route, then I would go the strong impervious route. That's what I decided then and ever after. I would be a survivor and deal with it later. Much later.

When my father died in 2017, it was over twenty years later. I realized how very much I'd held myself back from in my life in the very quiet name of fear. I held myself back from being a professional dancer, professional artist, doctor, or anyone who had a spotlight of any kind. Fear is quietly loud. It can be a silent killer if we allow it.

My choice to be a survivor is absolutely a big reason I'm still here. I covered my whole body under my parents' red and blue sleeping bag and hid my hair. Maybe he'd think I wasn't there, I'd think. It wasn't logical. Fear never is logical. It was most certainly warranted. He knew where I slept. If he chose to kill me, in the end, I knew he could have. I decided to survive, and to be hell bent on surviving even if it killed me. That irony was not lost on me.

That Friday evening before my own father died, I realized what fear had cost me. I realized what I had allowed fear to cost me. For more than twenty years I had been completely unwilling to acknowledge the depth and breadth of the fear of my stepfather. I was still terrified.

My fear was costly. I kept my oldest friend so far away that he didn't know how deeply I loved him. He never knew until decades later that I had been through anything that deeply changing or scary. I didn't even tell him I loved him, or how much. My ex-stepfather had said that he'd follow me to dance. He did follow me and drive by me several times when I walked that long wooded road to the dance studio after the bus dropped me off. He had been there, just like he said he would when he threatened to kill me. My fear asked why wouldn't he follow me to college, or to a family, to the love of my life?

He stayed far enough away that the restraining order wasn't violated. The very day it was up, my mother said he came up to her and stood next to her in the store for an uncomfortably long time. Two years later he had to prove that he was in control. Some people are too disturbed, too full of hatred, anger, or disfunction to see the light. In spite of what happened, I chose to be an active productive part of this beautiful world.

Some fears are very, very real, like this one. I'm very lucky to have survived that time. Still, I got to choose. I choose love. I choose light over darkness. I look for the good in others, who may be more challenging to appreciate. I choose to find their light. We all have outlets and things that feed our souls fire, our life force.

We may choose, despite the bad things, to love. It may not be innate or easy, but we are capable of choice. We can even choose to trust other humans in the face of someone completely breaking our trust in the past. We always choose how we react to a situation even if we do not have control over everything that ever happens to us.

Fear lies to you. Fear told me that hiding was safety. For all my hardened exterior, I had a very soft, very scared underbelly. I was so afraid that Nightmare Man would come back, I couldn't allow myself to love completely, or be loved unconditionally. I had too many unattainable conditions I placed on myself. Time and distance did not make it easier for me to trust people.

The opposite was actually true. It was much harder to open myself fully. I had to meet my own requirements before I would be worthy of love.

I lost the most important person in my life with that decision, myself. I lost myself when I allowed the fear to win and allowed the past to be more important than the present. I lost the present for twenty plus years to some extent.

I was almost thirty when I married. It took everything I had to step out onto the ledge and trust someone that much. It took that long for me to stop dating people I could 'fix' or 'help'. Before the incident, trust wasn't an issue because I was whole. After, I spent all my time looking for danger and waiting to be let down. Being in a relationship was like trying to run a marathon with a broken foot. The wounded animal in me couldn't expose my soft underbelly to them for long. Additionally, if I didn't allow myself to be at peace, then my ex-stepfather couldn't take away my happiness. I thought I was doing the people I loved a favor by protecting them. I also took away their ability to choose, and my chance at being happy. It took me a long time to realize that I deserved the partner, not the project. No one wants to be a project anyway.

Consequently, when I met someone I didn't have to fix, someone who was brilliant, driven, and intelligent with a huge heart, I did my absolute best to run away. Part of me knew though, deep inside, that I needed to trust in order to let go of the past. I wouldn't write about it in a journal. I wouldn't tell anyone. I did however, finally take that walk down the aisle. I reserved the right to watch out for that infamous other shoe, though. Life would find a way to test and retest that trust over the next decade.

My trust was well placed in my husband. He has taught me that it's okay to trust even if bad things have happened in the past. When trials and tribulations come, he stands firm on his grounding of love. Things aren't always easy, don't get me wrong. But there is so much light in the world when we are willing to see it.

I recently have been asking both myself and others who are brave enough to be early readers of this book for their thoughts. The first thirty pages were filled with all of the hardest things I was never willing to share, not even with my diary. They were the dark moments, the challenging ones, and the possible pitfalls of my life. Taken all at once, no one could finish the story. I knew there was a reason that would get to the heart of what needed to be said.

I asked the few brave souls what it was about the story that made it hard to stay the course. With something so personal it's hard to divorce yourself from the experience. While each thing could have broken me, I chose to find the light. I chose to create love, joy, and in most cases art of some form or another. But ask me to be objective about the history of my life and I'm stumped.

One person wisely said that those first chapters were like a marathon. "Give them some ice water once in a while to give them the strength to get to the finish line." Each of the big moments in my life is so intense in the retelling that I am transported back to the emotions, smells, sights, and sounds of each moment. From that perspective, I don't always know how it is for the reader.

My husband's advice was sage. "Don't water down your story. You write your story to cut it out of you, to lance the boil and be free. It's hard to read sometimes because it forces the reader to deal with their own fears. Fear is easily identifiable."

What I concluded on writing about fear was that watering it down would do others a disservice. I want people to know what it was like to be there in the room in those moments. I also want them to feel the triumph of choosing love, joy, or hope despite the harder times. How can you know what a triumph it is without knowing the moments I fell down or was tested? Removing the painful parts of my story would make the positive parts carry less weight somehow. What we do with our experiences becomes who we are. Who we choose to be in each situation then becomes what people remember of us when we're gone.

My mother never once complained about lung cancer or brain cancer or even her Chronic Obstructive Pulmonary Disease (COPD) that was really debilitating. She chose to be responsible for her past choices to smoke. She chose to find the joy in each moment even and especially when she was in physical discomfort. She even chose love, trust, and friendships after leaving my stepfather. Miracles aren't always what we think they are. But they do occur when we choose powerfully in spite of our fear. When we are brave, miracles are possible.

Giving in to my fear fed that wolf. Choosing that way became habit, so much so that I didn't realize I was afraid. Undoing old patterns took time and patience with myself. I had to look long and hard at situations. I had to be kind to myself when cycling through the decisions. It got easier. Before long, fear no longer ran the show. I did.

We are always bigger than we think we are. When we realize our own worth, then we know we can achieve our goals. I find that if I can get out of my own way, then big things happen. Being present and authentically you is the biggest gift you can give the world. Choose based on your fire not your fear.

Fear is not an enemy any more than grief. The key is to acknowledge the fear or grief and choose for myself.

Forgiveness

I realized that I didn't have to condone what had happened in order for her to be in our lives more intimately.

The word "forgiveness" was frankly vile to my ears and my heart for a long time. I stayed angry for many years over what happened, and what should have happened. I felt very alone in the world and unprotected. My teenage self would have laughed and walked out of the room if someone had told me I needed to forgive my mother.

Sometimes the solution is that you must separate to heal. I moved halfway across the country. My mother and I had a relationship as long as she didn't try to treat me like a child. I created boundaries that I needed at the time in order to have any relationship. It wasn't until the pain was less volcanically hot and I knew I was safe that I could even step into the room with the word forgiveness.

Deep down, underneath that vile pain was a child who knew how much my mother loved me. Somewhere, the logical part of me knew mistakes were made and she knew it. Deep down I wanted to forgive her. The time came in my mid-twenties that I tried to will myself to forgive her. It was as if I spoke abracadabra and expected it to simply happen. I felt like a failure when it didn't. She left my stepfather, annulled the marriage, and moved back home. She realized her mistakes. Wasn't it enough already? My teenage self didn't think so.

The breech in trust was so complete for me that I had no clue how to simply go back to the way things were before. I realize now that's not what happens with forgiveness. Again, I wish I could say there was an easy answer, but there simply isn't one. Perhaps sharing my road can lead people in the direction they want to go.

The day I found out I was pregnant, I tried on the word "mother." I had a good childhood honestly. There were great times before the incident. There were also tough times where I felt completely alone in the world. At one point I didn't know if I'd be murdered in my sleeping bag each night. Long after, my body remembered that traumatic experience. I didn't know if I wanted her in my child's life. I looked inward.

The first time I called myself a mother, I cringed. My picture of a mother was shattered at that time. It was not a pretty sight. I felt really justified in my pain and anger, too. I thought that somehow, I'd have to condone behaviors that hurt me in order to forgive. I had to first be honestly willing to choose to trust.

That first moment, it was as if I'd realized I needed glasses for the first time. When I was a child and put on my first pair, I saw the world clearly for the very first time. It reminded me of the *Wizard of Oz* movie when everything went full color. I asked myself some very important questions in order to decide what to do.

I asked myself: *Is she a danger to myself or my family? Is she still around him? Is he any more likely to come and kill me if she's in our lives more? Would she harm them? Would she love them? Do I want my child to have a grandmother?*

I had no clue how to do what I was proposing to myself. Yet, the answers to my questions were clear. My mother was not a danger to my family. She hadn't seen my ex-stepfather in more than a decade, since the restraining order. She would never harm my child, or any child, intentionally. She would love my child unconditionally, without reservation. It meant a lot to me that my child had a real family that included grandparents. Most importantly, I did not want my children to see life through the old faulty lenses that I had been seeing through!

If my answers to those questions were different then my choices would have been different as well. Putting a child in an unsafe situation is something that I would never do willingly. I had done my time separating with love. I had been solo trying to heal. Now I was entering a new phase.

I realized that I didn't have to condone what had happened in order for her to be in our lives more intimately. I was not saying it never happened, or even that my anger was wrong. I chose in that moment that my Mom and I could have a real honest relationship inside of motherhood. It gave us common ground that wasn't tainted by what had come before. I chose to let that be honest because I knew that children could always smell a lie. They would see that undertone of tension between us. I asked myself if I wanted that. I asked myself *who did I want to be as a mother?*

It was not a simple overnight snap of the fingers towards forgiveness for me. Not for this. However, when I chose to honestly let her be a part of my child's life, I chose forgiveness. I chose to be in the present moment talking about pregnancy nausea, stretch marks, and how the baby moved with the beat of the music. Every conversation got a bit easier. It happened in whispers over time.

My mother had apologized many times for what happened. Many times before, I knew to my core that she had meant it. And many times before, when I said I forgave her, it was a lie. I pretended I forgave her once she actually apologized because she meant it so sincerely. I pretended because I wanted it to be so, and it felt like the right thing to do.

One visit when my child was almost three years old, Mom came to spend some time with us. We had two

Forgiveness

children by that time and they called her Nanny. The children wore their child sized chef's hat and aprons. We made cookies together. The mess was all over the kitchen. The smile in our hearts was worth the clean up. That night, after they were asleep, she again said, "I'm so sorry for what happened. I never meant to hurt you." I had allowed her into my life and created an actual present tense relationship outside of that past pain. When I looked her in the eye and told her I forgave her, my body didn't cringe with a lie. It was the truth.

Finally, my body didn't recoil. Finally, anger didn't well up inside. Finally, I was free. I took a deep breath in and exhaled slowly with a smile. What I never realized until that moment was what freedom felt like as an adult. I heard the stories about how forgiveness gives more to you than you could ever imagine. Until that moment, I didn't really fully grasp how good it could feel.

As the years went on, the forgiveness didn't disappear. It stayed there. What's more, it got bigger and wider. I let her into my life more and more. By the time she moved near us in October of 2019, all that remained was love between us. We used our time wisely, all seven months of it. Counting the months, it seemed like the blink of an eye. And yet, standing in that hospital stirring her coffee, simply wondering if she'd enjoy it, it was worth the journey. The moments of thoughtful forgiveness had given rise to a future. We had a life together, she and I. We lived it well.

On her last Mother's Day, my children gave her a hand painted picture frame. It was a gift of the heart. On the wooden square frame, they inscribed words that embodied their Nanny. They wrote words like: "loving," "funny," "kind," "unique," "intelligent," "courageous," and "strong." The last two words really stuck with me, in particular. She was strong and courageous. Her grandchildren knew her as strong. She was always kind, but I wouldn't have always said she was strong. The important thing is that they saw her that way. What a gift that is to all of us! That's miraculous and more powerful than I can say. Her love was always present to anyone who knew her. Her quiet strength that came from deep inside was different. That was a trait she didn't boast about or flaunt. She earned it with time and experience.

Many of us would like to pretend that the pandemic didn't happen. Yet, it shaped us inextricably. It became synonymous with my mom's cancer journey for me as it happened simultaneously.

"Mom, you don't do anything small, do you? Metastatic cancer is big enough, but you have that during a global pandemic." I told her one day sitting in the van after picking up prescriptions. She belly laughed at my comment. Her laugh was raspy and usually made her cough. This time though, she just laughed, deeply. In that moment, she was free.

"No, I guess not," she said while laughing.

What do you do when you're faced with impossible odds? Ignore them, of course. Mom constantly said she was waiting for her miracle. There were so many her whole life though, that this would be no different. We did not live by the survival rates, the success rates of treatments, or what anyone told us. Thankfully, the doctors didn't tell us numbers either. Adenocarcinoma is no joke, but we had time. We didn't know how much, but we would use every single second wisely.

Forgiveness

The pandemic brought mortality to the forefront of many people's minds. She and I had faced mortality before, and everyone dies eventually. She'd just moved to be closer to me and my family. She wasn't going to waste any time with her grandchildren in the place she so loved.

Every single second we had before she died was well spent. She lived with us from October until mid-January. The apartment complex had originally told her there was an opening mid-October. Then they said, November, and December, and then finally January when she got in. We didn't let the changes get us down. We chose to use the time together under the same roof to make good memories.

The truth is no one knows when their last breath will be exactly. COVID-19 made us all aware of that. Then, add Mom's cancer on top like some ill-timed cherry and you have the last year of our lives. Mom and I laughed a lot. She may not have died of COVID but she's connected to it intimately. We had the hard-earned ability to speak openly between us. She wasn't living for the numbers or the odds. She lived for the miracles of possibility. Mom and I knew we had very little time. We chose to be real, honest, and to do the big things and enjoy every moment. I'm forever grateful that we had the time.

In the last four years my family lost three out of the four grandparents. My dad lived with us for five years before dying in 2017. Six months later, my father-in-law, who had beaten lung cancer and survived a massive stroke, passed in his mid-eighties. In 2020, my mom was newly diagnosed with lung cancer. The blessing is that my children knew them all. The pain comes with that too. However, they weren't just names to my children. They were people. Silver lining.

The Thursday before Mom died, she said, "I've done everything I can think to do, what's left? Why am I still here?" Despite treatment, the three tumors in her brain would certainly grow again. More immediately, a tumor was wrapped around the artery inside her lung, piercing through it. On top of that, she caught pneumonia. Breathing had been quite a struggle. That struggle came like an impossibly fast runaway freight train. Lung radiation helped her breathing to come easier. That was a blessing. She was peaceful and calm. She honestly wanted to know what she had left to do. Mom had deep faith and believed that if she was still on the Earth then she had something yet to do.

"Mom, you've done the work of your life. Last Saturday you had a window to go. You were not ready. Don't underestimate the power of the human will," I told her. "You'll get another window. I don't know when it will be but you can make another choice when it comes."

Choice matters. God's timing and our bodies' capacities matter a lot, of course. But sometimes in the darkest moments people forget that human will and free choice is a real thing.

Everyone's line in the sand is different. Watching my mother suffer, prying the BiPap breathing machine off her face every thirty seconds to suction the foamy bloody sputum from her lungs was harder than most could imagine. She didn't have the strength to cough let alone pry that huge thing off her face. She did it anyway. If you've borne witness to strength like that, then you know that you are forever changed by the experience. In fact, I would say that we are all changed

Forgiveness

by the experiences we go through. Who we choose to be in each moment matters. When Mom was suffering that Saturday, she firmly said "I have to try."

She was referring to lung radiation and fighting the cancer. The tumor in her lung was tearing her blood vessels and closing her airway. She could barely breathe. **And** she chose to fight. She fought for my children, her grandbabies. She fought for her family at large. She fought to prove to herself she was capable of fighting. She chose of her own free will and surprised herself by that choice. That next week they did lung radiation and she got weaker and weaker. She couldn't walk, stand, or get out of bed, but she breathed easier. They eased her suffering in a very real way. Her joy was not diminished, extinguished, or dimmed in any way. In fact, her light, peace, and love grew stronger until her failing body could no longer hold her soul of light.

That Saturday we had the hospice conversation for the first time. She equated hospice with death and didn't want to equate herself with death. However, while there was resistance there, she boldly realized that hospice was honestly her best chance of survival. She explored her inner feelings, stigmas, and prejudices on the matter that came from being a former nurse. I reminded her that she was more than welcome to get kicked out of hospice for doing too well. I fully knew she wouldn't get kicked off even though my father-in-law had miraculously done just that with stage four lung cancer. I knew her time to go home to God was close. Still, I was present in each moment and able to make her laugh and just be there for her for whatever she needed. The time we spend with our loved ones, loving them, is always time well spent, even if it's hard.

One day that last week, a woman from the cafeteria brought Mom coffee. It was hot, bless her. She'd brought sugar and cream as Mom requested. I quietly stood up and asked Mom how she wanted her coffee that day. I guessed the answers, but I still asked. I gave her the choice. I looked up at her and realized as if outside myself that while she was very definitely dying, I was just a loving daughter stirring her coffee in that moment. It's so very rare to be able to be fully present while someone is dying. It's even more rare if there's been a huge break in trust like I'd had with Mom defending the man who wanted to kill me as a teenager. The precious, undeniable, beautiful gift that both Mom and I had was time, true forgiveness, and in the last months being fully present with each other.

It was a miracle that I had forgiven her for not protecting me. It was a miracle that I had any relationship with her at all. The healing that forgiveness brought to both our lives was immeasurable. From that first moment I knew I was pregnant with my first child, I wasn't sure how I felt about her role in his life. Fear doesn't have a stopwatch and it doesn't just magically stop one day. We have to choose to stop our own watch, little by little.

It became clear to me that my fear sprung from experiences that happened many years ago. I could choose differently when I could see clearly what I had been choosing all those years. Like anything of that magnitude, that journey is ongoing and ever evolving.

Looking back, it reminds me of the way my astrologer father talked about Pluto. "The cycle of Pluto takes twenty-eight years," he'd say. "You keep cycling the same issues but are ever evolving upward, albeit slowly. When you look back at the beginning, from the end of that journey only then can you see how far you've come."

Each and every one of the baby steps I took from that point led me towards forgiveness and healing from that old pain. My mother was full of love and light. She also had deep regrets and her own demons to overcome. She worked so very hard to do just that before the end.

What changed? Was she sorrier this time? No. Was she stronger, different, or somehow more than she was when she first said she was sorry? Yes. She had grown some but that wasn't why I'd forgiven her. It was only recently when my husband asked me "Did fear hold you back from forgiving her?" that I realized it had. Fear was the key. All these years I've wondered and been honestly plagued by it. I felt bad for saying I forgave her but not meaning it wholeheartedly. I'd been willing, but my heart hadn't completed that job. In the walking of each step away from the glasses of the past, I was able to see clearly that the present was different. Choice became mine once again.

Forgiveness doesn't happen outside of ourselves. It happens in our own hearts as a product of our choices. Some things are a lot bigger than the words "I'm sorry." When we choose powerfully, honestly, and from a place of integrity rather than an old story, then we are free. We all have histories. Some of our stories cut deeper than others. But you can't have history without story. Or can you? It is possible to have a history without wearing the story of the past on your heart every single day. Those chains I wore were so heavy!

That day I looked at her and realized I had finally forgiven her. I could breathe deeply around her. I was able to be present for her, to listen to wherever she was right then without what happened decades ago overshadowing the moment. Living today, thriving in today, becomes possible when we are able to be completely present. I could not be present with my mother until I was able to forgive her. I couldn't forgive her until I was willing to take one step at a time. One of the greatest blessings of my life is forgiving her. We completed all our old stories with each other. We turned the pages on our history. Sometimes they came up and we dealt with them. The biggest miracle with my mother was that I had one as an adult.

The year 2020 was one of evolution, grief, and inner work for most of us on this planet, whether we liked it or not. We've all dealt with it in the best way we know how. For me, it was imperative to be fully present with Mom. We were going to suck the marrow out of life, like Thoreau's students, first and foremost. We accomplished that mission like two children with joy and love. Talk about a miracle!

At the end of each day beginning March of 2020, I was utterly exhausted. I put aside all of my feelings on her illness, the what ifs, the worries, the sorrow, and the despair. Instead, we went to lunch after a doctor's appointment and reveled in how delightful the Mediterranean bowl tasted. Being present takes effort and constant choice. Sometimes a year, a month, a week, or even a day is far too long. Instead, it becomes a question of which wolf will you feed every second? Mom and I chose to feed the Light. We did things she wanted to do, ate where she wanted to eat, and talked a lot about all of it. We chose to feed joy and love. We chose faith in God's timing and the ultimate journey. We chose to believe in miracles regardless of odds or

Forgiveness

how many tumors there were. We chose well. I'll never be sorry.

It wasn't a lie or inauthentic. I asked myself that question constantly. We simply chose to treat each day as a gift, as we're all meant to anyway. By choosing to focus on the positive, we created more positive. We chose the unreasonable because it brought us joy. I supported her goals and joys. We bought furniture for her apartment in January and she died in June. But her books made it to those shelves, and she loved every minute of feeling at home. She deliberately chose not to wait around to die no matter how much or how little time she had left. There's a lot of life to be lived in the times of waiting.

Other than "I love you," the most important thing I think I could've told her was that she had done the business of her life before it was her time to go. It wasn't a lie either. She had come out of that marriage in the 1990s battered and bruised and terrified. It was easier for her to forgive other people than to forgive herself. Mom made friends with forgiveness. She courted it quietly, one piece at a time.

She died a beautiful butterfly with many friends, fully emerged. She didn't have any skeletons in her closet. She had not let fear win. She won. Mom won each and every moment of her life by living it fully, to the last drop.

Mom was looking for her miracle, but didn't quite catch it. The miracles were everywhere though. She overcame many mountains in her lifetime and still chose love. She loved her animals as if they were people. Some may say she loved them more than people because they didn't ever hurt you. They were safe. Mom said they always chose love.

Forgiveness is more than uttering the words "I forgive you." Forgiveness is like the mighty old oak tree. It begins as a tiny acorn, blown with the wind. The acorn must first crack that hard protective shell for the roots to plunge into the rich earth. Sunlight warms the sapling and the water nourishes it. We want forgiveness to be fast. Like most things, we want it to be easy. I wanted my willingness to be enough, but I needed much more than that. I needed safety, something honest to share with her, and a launching pad.

Forgiving my mother gave me one.

Forgiveness is more than uttering the words "I forgive you." We want forgiveness to be fast. Like most things, we want it to be easy. I wanted my willingness to be enough, but I needed much more than that.

Mom's Journey

The truth is that without the pain, you may not really respect or love the respite and the joy. There's a lot of life to be lived in the times of waiting.

From her birth in 1946 to her death in 2020, Mom had great triumphs. It wasn't all rocky. She would want all of us to focus there, in fact. The truth is that without the pain, you may not really respect or love the respite and the joy. She experienced life fully.

Her first major accomplishment was graduating high school. She had children at a young age. During the Vietnam War, when she almost died having her second child because he was breach, she didn't let the Red Cross call her husband home from Germany. She was afraid his duty station would be switched to Vietnam if he came home. She was thinking of his well-being, rather than her own. I'm sure she was terrified. Several years later, when it was no longer healthy for her to remain in the marriage, she left to protect herself and her children. That was no small feat at that time. Mom went on to work full time in the Operating Room as an OR tech cleaning the tools in the autoclave and assisting. She graduated from Nursing School with her RN degree. She worked hard to earn that degree and get pinned. Her parents helped with the children while she worked fiendishly to give them a better life. That's the truth. She is the first in her family of that generation to graduate High School, the first to go to college and the first to graduate. She loved people deeply in her lifetime. She loved animals even more, if one could believe that. It was a miracle that Mom loved deeply and authentically until the day she died, despite the trauma she'd endured.

Through it all, my mother maintained eternal optimism. She married three times in her life. The second marriage was to my father. They met on common ground at the same church but evolved separately when my dad got sober. They loved each other until the day they each died. She said her third husband, my ex-stepfather, was like a mid-life crisis mistake. The optimist in her saw the light inside someone who wasn't feeding that light.

I believe with all my heart that every step of my mother's last months was miraculous. She was able to leave the cold weather of New York state behind, which was not good for her COPD lung condition, move to be near grandchildren who loved her dearly, and to let go of the past that she would not let define her. The journey took more than a few months, you understand. Her life's work, in fact, was rising above every single thing that some may say Satan threw at her. She rose to the occasion not with the Huron Indian war club her grandmother had. Mom rose like the wind, slow and steady like the turtle, with the loyalty of a saint. She was an angel, like Mr. Godsend said. She wasn't perfect, but she rose to the occasion of her life after enduring many trials and was reborn.

Mom's passing and her last week were full of more miracles. She'd never considered the possibility she would not beat the cancer, let alone that she'd die, until the week before she passed. It shocked her, like finding your true hair color was brown after being blonde for decades. Mom spent that last week preparing for her passing. She talked to everyone she could, in short spurts between the BiPap and the suction and fifteen liters of oxygen. She inspired the nurses, doctors, and herself that week. She also inspired me. It was a whirlwind week full of authenticity, lessons, and love.

Through it all Mr. Godsend was there, with the exact right prayers via text. He solidified the 'we' and 'us' concept of unifying humanity rather than dividing them by color or race. After she passed, I sent a photo of Mom holding a baby wild squirrel, and he said it was "proof she'd been an angel on earth." Lord, the things that angel walked through in her lifetime! But the words rang true that day. I was grateful for them.

I will always be grateful for completing that heart mission, forgiving her. What a segue right? Well, my thoughts bounced back to my teenage years and her annulled marriage when he called her an angel. Even in the face of the memory, I believed him wholeheartedly! That's true forgiveness. Most importantly, it was authentic and real. That's a miracle too!

The morning of her discharge from the hospital, we both felt excited. I could see Mom had perked up after her week-long stay and the medical procedures that were necessary but not fun. The Occupational Therapist (OT) and Physical Therapist (PT) had to sign off on her release. "Walk for me," the PT said. Mom practically jumped out of bed and over to her walker. She walked with a pep in her step fifteen feet one way, turned around, and walked right back just as fast. She was visibly winded sitting down in the white hospital bed afterwards. It was only a few minutes later, the OT came and had her go to the bathroom. The job of the OT was to determine if Mom would be safe to go home. Occupational Therapists wear a lot of hats involving many activities of daily living from swallowing to getting to the bathroom safely. As a former Registered Nurse, Mom knew that if she made it to the bathroom and back on her own that she would be released. A little more tired, she got up and walked the five feet to the bathroom toilet and then back once finished. The cardiologist signed her release papers and we were out

Mom's Journey

of there!

Later, in the week of her passing, the kind cardiologist said, "I knew she was pushing herself too hard. But who was I to keep her from going home?" When I asked him to give it to me straight, he graciously took the time to do so with compassion. That same man prayed with her at the end, and effectively gave her last rights. Words can never express the gift he gave my mother and our family. He let her go home to say goodbye to her beloved cat, Meg. He let her say goodbye to her life, to grieve the apartment she'd just set up. And yes, he followed every medical rule and procedure. They even did a chest x-ray before releasing her and checked her vitals including temperature. She passed the tests on her own accord, fair and square.

Mom had a great medical team of doctors that followed her in the hospital. For a myriad of reasons, doctors in the hospital are strangers to you, the patient, and maybe to each other. It seems like they don't always talk to one another. Each hospital is different with different skill sets. The hospital policy let you have your personal doctors if they had privileges there. So, she was followed by her pulmonologist, her cardiologist, her oncologist, and her radiologist. The cardiologist and pulmonologist actually talked with each other and discussed her treatment plan like she was their mother. At the end, when Mom's vitals were not staying up anymore and she'd been on the BiPAP mask with high flow oxygen for more than a week, the pulmonologist was kind and spoke straight to her.

She asked him, "What do you think my prognosis is?"

He paused for a moment and replied, "It is

unfortunate. But I know that you know we are not meant to live forever. We will do what we can for you to make you comfortable."

Keep in mind that Mom had already talked with him about how she felt, her faith, and her wishes. He knew her and had a rapport with her, even in the short time she had been his patient. She had metastatic lung cancer in two places, with three tumors in her brain. The tumor in her left lung had cut off her airway and into the artery in her lung at that point. Suffering doesn't even begin to describe it. This and many other reasons are why people say, "cancer sucks." The pulmonologist was a kind, gentle soul who fought hard in the ICU for many patients, including my mother. These doctors were her guardian angels, the protectors of her precious life to the best of their ability. I know they took that Hippocratic oath very seriously. The best gifts they gave us was their honesty, integrity, knowledge, and their hearts.

Speaking as someone who wanted to be a doctor more than anything in the world, I can tell you that most people go into medicine because they do profoundly want to help people. They each have their why, as with any profession. They, much like teachers, have a special calling. The system isn't perfect; we all know that. But the souls of medical professionals are, in large part, as genuine and good as the men and women that cared for Mom. We, as patients, may not always see that. But usually their hearts are in the right place.

After her week and a half hospital stay, she came home for twenty-four hours. She hit the brain radiation wall when we pulled into the apartment complex. That infamous wall is one that many people have heard about but may not understand until they see it. When you know, you know.

We were released at 11:30 A.M. and I asked where she wanted to go.

"I'd love some good food," she gushed and then asked with trepidation, "Mediterranean?" She never wanted to burden anyone or ask them to do too much for her.

"That sounds great Mom," I said. We got our Mediterranean bowls with rice, quinoa, grilled chicken, tomatoes, tzatziki, cucumbers, and olives. We knew it could be her last meal, but we'd secretly felt that way for months. We indulged and got what she wanted, living in the moment. That day, the weight was heavy. The veil was off and she was tired. She'd had her first hospitalization since the cancer diagnosis and it was hard on her. She never gave up though. Never.

"Can we stop at the house so the kids can give you a hug?" I asked. What I didn't say was louder than my question. I'm sure she knew.

"Sure, we can. I'd like that" she said. She stayed in the van and they came out and hugged her and spent a few precious moments with her in the driveway and the sunshine. I took photos, even though Mom had newly gained fifty pounds of fluid. You never know. That was their last hug. I lived for the moment but hadn't given up hope.

Before Mom moved down, my gut told me that time with her would be short. I took the time to say things I may not have said, to spend time I didn't have, and loved like it was the last day I'd have with her. My dad always said, "you never regret the time you spent with people. You regret what you don't do." Brilliant to the last drop, that man. That day as I drove her home, all I was thinking was that my children needed to hug her, to see her, to touch her. They needed to know she was alive today. Today mattered.

The two-mile drive from my home to her apartment felt like forever. I could see how tired she was. We didn't talk about that. She was going home. Her home was safe. Her home was clean. Her home was hers and how she wanted it. I pulled the van up slowly to the overhang in the front of the building, and put it in park. I got out her red and black walker with the seat, set it up, and opened her door. I held onto the walker's handle for dear life. Thank the Lord my EMT training didn't vanish into the ether. She plopped down hard into that seat with zero energy. She fell down so hard that the seat backed up several inches even with my death grip on the handle. She didn't fall onto the concrete, thankfully. But I instantly knew I was in trouble.

She had gone from smiling with the glint in her eyes, to one hundred percent empty in an instant. The brain radiation finally caught up with her even though she ran as fast as she could to stay ahead of it. She walked as far as the apartment twenty-five feet from the van and that was it. She took her last steps heading home to a place she was so proud of having created. She had the Mediterranean bowl she loved one more time. She said goodbye to Meg, her fourteen-year-old Maine Coon cat that last night home.

That night, I stayed up with her because she coughed for four hours straight. I wore my mask while in the room with her. She had tested negative for COVID once already with the rapid test. She couldn't breathe but wouldn't complain. She worried about me sleeping enough. That was her way. That last twenty-four hours she was home, I was in way over my head. I knew it from the moment we got out of the van. And, I let her have her moment at home, her dignity.

Around 10:00 AM the next morning, the home nurse came and quickly realized Mom needed to go back to the hospital. The couch cushions and pillows I'd propped her up with weren't enough to help her breathe anymore. Truth be told they were never enough. We both knew it. Still, we tried.

I knew the day she was diagnosed, and the rainbows and ladybugs came from heaven, that she'd join my father all too soon. My friend Lisa knew too but she dreamt with me and held me up so I could hold up Mom during her journey. I am forever indebted to her for that. St Patrick's Day had many rainbows that year. I guess the ladybug and my friendships are the pot of gold.

God, the Universe, Buddha, the great Spirit, knew I needed some monumental strength to walk with Mom through her journey. From the moment of her diagnosis, Mom said she was "ready for her miracle." That statement would evolve into "someone will have a miracle from this. I'm just not sure if it's me." Every step of Mom's journey was a miracle that started before she moved here to be with us.

The first miracle was the apartment's timing. We were told she'd get an apartment on October fifteenth. So, I rushed between volunteer events and life to pack up her things and move her South.

The second miracle was her letting go of the last bit of stuff that consumed her in that apartment. She'd been a borderline hoarder. That had slowly improved until her personal D-day came: packing day. Several of her friends, her brother, and I came together to help pack her items the storage container. My job was to get her to decide what went in because there wasn't enough room for everything she didn't need. Every single item pained her to let go of, but she knew the time had come, and rose to the task. She was going to the beach, her Mecca. She did the job at hand triumphantly and painstakingly through the dust. More than once I had my hand on the phone to call 911 because she wasn't breathing well. But she completed the mission. She got rid of enough so that we were able to fit everything in the storage container. She purged just enough that the last box of books, coin bin, antique furniture, and dumpster dive furniture alike all fit. It all fit in the container.

We celebrated by going to an Indian restaurant downtown. It was fabulous. My packing partner was a treasure that day, much like the rest of Mom's community had been for years. Taking him to dinner was a small gesture of thanks, much like the flowers we gave to another couple who helped. Their gifts of time were priceless for all of us. That was early October, 2019.

I came home from that moving trip so different for many reasons. Years of clutter had come to a close. I got Mom out of that state like she'd wanted for years. We were leaving the past in the past. We traveled bravely down the road, excited and nervous like two school girls.

In the days since Mom passed, we packed and emptied her apartment, sorted through every stitch of everything again, and separated it into piles. Less than a year went by between moving her closer and packing up her things after she died. It was deeply emotional work that took more than I had some days. I gave it my all because I was on an unseen deadline. I didn't know what it was, but I could sense it coming.

We have all been through things in this life. Most of us have lost those we loved. What would your people say to you if they could? I bet they'd say they loved you and that they were proud of you. They'd probably say that you did the best you could. If you needed a swift kick in the pants maybe they'd add that too. Most likely though, they'd hug you and tell you how special you were to them. My mom would tell us to "trust the process. Trust it like I did in the end. Know that you're on the just right path for you. If you fall, get back up. You can do it. You've got what it takes to succeed. The Universe will provide the wind for your sails at the exact right time for you. Have faith."

Mom's passing was as one of a kind as her life. She lived on her terms once she gave herself permission. She had a childlike wonder, an artist's eye, and a survivor's heart. Witnessing someone dying is sad. It is so much more than that as well. Walking the end of life with someone isn't a burden. It is bearing witness to something so much larger than us. My parents were very different people. So, accordingly, their journeys home were polar opposites.

Love does not wither on some imaginary vine when someone's body dies. Love is eternal.

 *Love does not wither on some imaginary vine when someone's body dies. Love is eternal.*

I Gotta Pee

Unwanted situations are often our greatest teachers. Total control is a fallacy.

Who knew that a tiny unseen invader would be the fight of my life? I did have a feeling that I'd likely get the virus since I was my mom's transportation to all her doctor's appointments during the Pandemic. What I didn't see coming was that it would be the biggest battle I'd faced yet. That's saying something.

The first signs of illness were subtle like the wind. From the first serious sign and symptoms this felt different than anything I'd ever faced. Maybe time will tell that they weren't connected. I'm not sure. Here they are regardless. My throat was sore in the normal way it can be at the beginning of an illness. Mom's ER Dr. called me since I wasn't allowed into the hospital because Mom had respiratory symptoms. She'd seen Mom the first admittance too. She told me to stay away for three days or so if I could and see how I felt. So, I stayed at Mom's apartment for a couple of very long days. I continued drinking at least two peppermint-cinnamon-lemon teas per day and added an antioxidant pomegranate juice per day as a precaution and immune booster.

When the three quarantine days were up, I'd rested more and felt fine again. So, I went home to my family. I began visiting Mom a couple hours a day with my mask on faithfully each time. I was allowed in because she'd tested negative a second time for COVID with the rapid one-and-a-half-hour test. The ER doctor did let me know that the rapid COVID tests had twenty-five percent false negative rates. 2020 was a year of being in hibernation and perpetual change for a lot of us.

Each day I faithfully used my protocol from my EMT and pre-med days. I'd mask up like hospital regulations asked of me and go up to Mom's room taking care not to touch too many things. Sanitizer went on my hands before I entered her room, every time I touched something, on the way out, and again at the car before driving home. I was an EMT before I got married, I could do this, I told myself. Upon returning home, I took my shoes off in the garage, washed my hands thoroughly as well as the mask (being careful not to touch things or set it down beforehand), and stripped to my underwear in the kitchen. My clothing immediately went straight into the washer, so no one touched it. I went up and showered, hugged my babies only after I was clean, and spent time with my family. Sleep. Repeat.

That protocol continued until she died. Each day, I thanked the Universe that I had another day on this Earth and could breathe freely and deeply.

My next symptoms I wrote off as dealing with the dust of moving and sorting. My lungs hurt. It was again subtle. It was there at the same time our friend Dennis got sick after Father's Day, and then again when John got sick July 3rd. Then, there we were July 19th at 4:50 AM. I got tested on Friday at the naval hospital after a disturbingly dismissive phone call referral requirement. Being an active-duty member's dependent, I had to call the military COVID hotline. The hotline nurse checked "no known exposure," after a few painful sentences. Across the hall from Mom was a known COVID case. I overheard the nurse telling the doctor before the doctor entered the other room. I knew it wasn't her fault that she had to check that box. It felt untrue though, in the moment. The nurse on the phone had nothing to do with the years of unfeeling, dismissive healthcare that a lot of military dependents faced daily. Regardless, I got the required referral to be tested. Then, we waited.

The acute, noticeable symptoms were severe sore throat, runny nose, fever of 100.9, chills, body aches that made walking intensely painful, and the lung pain. The fever and chills came and went. The body aches were less over time. I slept for most of two weeks. It was painful to talk. It felt like someone poured acid down my throat.

My regimen was three teas a day and a super antioxidant drink two times a day plus rest, good food, and extra vitamin C. My mother-in-law sent Mom a memory foam wedge I slept on so I didn't choke on my own fluids. That was a terrifying and scary experience I'd prefer not to repeat. Swallowing was like tearing my throat in half each time.

How many times a day do you swallow? I wondered I was currently trying to quit. I avoided swallowing like the plague, pun intended.

I also sought out the light in people, situations, and in every moment. I was positive even though like many others at the time, I had been waiting to get it and die. It was more like an intense fear. I worked hard not to let it ruin our lives.

Good lord, if COVID knew what we'd been through the last six years alone, it would skip our house. COVID would say, "no, no, that home, that family has suffered enough." But it does not work like that. COVID isn't sentient or political even if we are fools acting like it is. The arrogance of humanity that we don't see is that A, historically and scientifically we were overdue for a pandemic and B, that COVID is a blind, ruthless killer like cancer.

Two weeks had gone by with me disconnected from my life, lying in bed asleep twenty-two out of twenty-four hours. The sunlight beamed in strongly by the time my eyes opened for the first time. My body reminded me to sit up slowly with dizziness and the black spots in my peripheral vision. Taking small steps, coughing, and grabbing onto the dresser first and then the walls, I made my way methodically to the bathroom. The doorway opened up into the view of the toilet and 1980s style vanity. Hiding the olive green original tiles was a single piece of light tan Berber carpet. My lungs burned as I gasped for air, coming to a stop at the toilet. I gazed out the window and smiled wearily at the sunlight beaming through the green maple leaves. The delicate leaves gently rustled in the breeze.

My hands shook. It must've been a long time since I'd eaten last. Slowly (always slowly!) I made my way downstairs to the kitchen. Our two beautiful babies ran to hug me. Sucking in the air as my body allowed, I held my breath. I didn't want to breathe on them lest I get them sick. My whole body rocked side to side as they each collided into my arms. Joy flooded my heart as I held on tight. They didn't know it but my son and daughter held me up in those moments.

Everything took longer. It wasn't a matter of choice. It was a necessity. Eating peanut butter on toast took all the energy I had for the day. Taking small bites and breathing in between made the world feel like it was moving in supersonic speed. I felt like I was in slow motion.

Exhausted, my right foot set down on the first stair step. My legs felt like lead weights, I thought. My left foot went down on the second step. The stairway started closing in on me and I was gasping for air. At the third step I stopped, bent over and gasped. My visual field was closing in and I couldn't catch my breath. So, I waited. I breathed. In time, the breathing eased and slowed. I took the next step and the next. The experience was teaching me something. *What was it?* I asked myself. Looking up at the top of the staircase, I could not see the top landing. *Where was it?*

I had faith that it was there. I'd seen it hundreds of times before. Today, this staircase felt insurmountable. I knew deep down that I could climb these stairs. Today, it would just take longer. Time was now officially fired. I could not look at a clock on my phone and climb the stairs. I could not count the seconds. I could only hold the railing like it was the last one on earth and climb one step at a time.

Crap! I thought. Dad's right again. "Surrender to win," he had said. One step at a time I would. I first had to believe that I could. That day and for quite a while, I climbed on faith.

The wooden floorboards were a golden oak color running left to right in the hallway, perpendicular to the stairs. It drew my eye into the bedroom and the bed to my left. Sigh. *I can do this.* With all the concentration of a deep breathing yoga exercise, I caught my breath for the final push to the bed. Once my vision came back from seeing the stars, I began walking slowly and with purpose. This was the last bit. Then I could rest. Huff and puff. No grandmother's house and no big bad wolf were here today. Huff and puff. One more. Finally, I made it to the bed. The gray fluffy blanket was so soft and welcoming. I was drenched in sweat and quaking head to toe. I knew this feeling. It was complete muscle exhaustion. Yet, I simply climbed the stairs. That was enough.

My hazel eyes drifted towards the pulse oximeter on the nightstand. I had inherited it a month before when

I Gotta Pee

my mother passed away. *I feel just like my mother,* I thought. *I am me,* I retorted in my head as I put the pulse oximeter onto my pointer finger and sat down on the edge of the bed.

What?! Eighty? That can't be right! Switching fingers did not help bring that number higher. Only time would bring the number closer to the goal. One hundred percent was the best number one could see there glowing red from the little rectangular instrument. That meant that all of your blood was oxygenated. You wouldn't see stars or lose your breath at one hundred percent. I took that number for granted just seconds ago, it seemed. I was in a new reality now. This reality was like the twilight zone to me. *It was temporary.* I would tell myself that until I believed my own words.

Settling into bed, I pulled the covers over my shoulders. The memory foam wedge was a love it, hate it device. If I laid flat, I could not breathe. If I laid on the wedge, I was up at a forty-five-degree angle and didn't choke quite as much. My lungs were aching more. I coughed until I could not see light. Then I unwrapped a cough drop with my pale hands shaking so much that I dropped the darn thing. I scooped it back up and set it in my mouth. The quicks of my fingernails were blue. Not good. I knew I should go to the hospital but didn't want to. No, I knew I couldn't. Breathing in the eucalyptus scent, the cough eased. I laid down as if there were unhatched eggs beneath me. Any faster and more pain would come.

Sleep came like a restless lover at night. During the day though, I was so weary that as soon as my eyes closed, I was gone. Dreams would not come, or be remembered. Sometimes when I woke, I wasn't sure I was still alive. That particular day, I wasn't sure I could fight anymore.

The pressure from my bladder stirred me from deep sleep. What did it take to be in a coma? I had to be close. I knew that breathing was involuntary. However, I had to tell my body to breathe when I was awake. The drive to breathe was so low. I'd take deep breaths knowing that I'd cough like a madwoman just to remember I could sometimes. Not that day though. I had nothing left. No. Energy. At All.

Without opening my eyes, I debated. I could go right here. It would be so easy to just let go. I don't have to fight anymore. I was clear that I didn't have it in me anyway. It took great effort to inhale and exhale. It took effort to breathe, effort to sleep, and insurmountable effort to get to the bathroom. I could give up, I thought. Giving up would have been far easier than fighting.

Laughter downstairs broke my thoughts. They must be watching cartoons again. My daughter and son were laughing. *Really?!* I scolded myself silently. *You're going to give up now? Now? You fought like hell, so those children had a father, a whole intact father and you're going to give up? No way, Jose! You fought hard to stay alive, fought a dangerous criminal masquerading as your stepfather. You won. You survived. And you're going to leave those babies now? I don't think so. Get your ass up and go pee.*

Man, my inner dialogue can be rough sometimes. It worked. In a split second, I knew. I was not going to let this invisible virus take me willingly. I would continue to fight. "I gotta pee," I said out loud to no one. It was my battle cry, my war cry. It was my F.U. to the germs that threatened my life. Not willingly. You'll have to fight harder. I'm not leaving this family. This is not my time.

Getting to the bathroom was every bit as tiring as it had been that morning, and yet, my Soul Fire had returned. I was staying here, if I could help it. God may have other plans. Lord knows that. If he did, I would accept that. I would not give up on my family, however. A slow smile spread across my bed sheet wrinkled face as I sat there. For the first time, I could see tomorrow through the lens of today. I had hope.

Each and every day I rose. I was unstoppable because this illness would not beat me, regardless of the outcome. I made two beautiful, intelligent children and did my best to create art, joy, and love wherever I went. I would continue to do so until my last breath, however long that may be.

I rise because if none of the other things I've encountered have killed me, I won't lie down and let this one kill me either. I will rise as sure as the sun does, albeit later than the sun usually, and do my best to be a light in this world. **My light will not be hidden anymore.**

It was only a month since Mom died when I got COVID. I asked myself more than once, *how am I still here?* I was simultaneously presented with my own ego asking, "how could this happen to me," and the very real fire inside my soul that said, "I will not make it easy for COVID to take me down." Why? How am I the optimist? How is it that I don't just give up when things keep happening to me or my family?

I was trained to look for the good in people in small ways and large. As a young child, I felt love overflowing. The love poured into me became the fuel for my soul's fire. Finding, listening to, and sometimes creating your own deep inner knowing takes something. It's an undertaking worth investing in.

I almost died. The virus was still new. Vaccines weren't created yet. My body didn't recognize it as an enemy until it was almost too late. My tonsils were so swollen that my airway was nearly completely obstructed. They oozed and dripped into my aching pneumonia-riddled lungs. At the time I got the virus, they were intubating people and putting them on ventilators. The medical community thought then that this would allow people to heal. I knew that I would never make it off a ventilator. My whole body was inflamed, especially my throat. My lungs were so tired that each breath I took required all the energy I had. For two weeks I slept all but two hours a day.

As far as Soul Fire was concerned, my life force, it was near totally extinguished. I had two sticks to rub together. They barely made a spark. When my children laughed downstairs, I heard my why. In a flash, I went through everything I'd faced until that point. I got up and went to the bathroom rather than slip into a coma.

Medically speaking, I would never recommend doing what I did without a hospital. I also know for myself, during that time, I did the right thing for me. I did what I could do to fight it off at home, without a ventilator. I almost lost the ability to choose one way or another, mind you. Thankfully, my immune system kicked into high gear.

I have always been healthy. Perhaps, I even took that fact for granted. COVID humbled me. I nearly lost my life to it. We cancelled my mother's funeral twice because I was so sick. It wasn't safe. The day that the pain finally lessened in my throat, I made the call. I was awake for longer than I'd been in a month. My throat felt only a tiny bit better. I knew that meant that I had a chance to make it. I set the funeral date a third time. It was a month away.

I looked at my husband that day and told him. "I set the funeral date for Mom. It's an outdoor funeral. We will either bury two bodies or three. By then, I'll either be dead, or no longer contagious." We were burying my parents together at the same time even though Dad passed years prior. He looked at me incredulously. He didn't understand. He never realized how close I got to that cliff. He couldn't go there. I knew. I had danced with death practically my whole life. When it came knocking for me, I shut the door in Death's face. Not yet.

I'm grateful to not be buried beside my parents right now. They have a beautiful bronze headstone in a very peaceful cemetery. I'm not chomping at the bit to join them. After breathing through a straw for a month while fighting COVID, I'm grateful and determined to follow my path and do the work of my life.

Total control is a fallacy. I blindly went through life, not thinking about my own death. I was young, healthy, and in the middle of raising children. I kept other people alive, like my husband. Not the other way around. Circumstances forced me to look at my own mortality. Irony put me in the situation. I swore to myself that I would not deliberately smoke, like my mother. I swore that I wouldn't be the one huffing and puffing to get up the stairs. Here I was anyway. Thanks, Irony.

Unwanted situations are often our greatest teachers. I had to retrain my brain, refocus, and recenter myself. My life was different now. I didn't ask for it. I didn't cause it. I didn't want it. It wasn't even emotionally based. It was medically based. There was a slew of emotions to wade through, including grief. I wasn't the same after getting sick. My whole body was filled with inflammation. All my body systems came very close to shutting down. I had to heal.

I had been caught off guard. That was unusual. Everything I knew about my body was thrown out the window. I had to learn on the fly. I had to take each day as it came. There was no rule book, no handbook, no medical dictionary for what I would face. All my years studying science, biology, and the human body did not prepare me for what came next.

I wasn't totally empty handed. I had my faith that the top of the stairs existed no matter how long it took me to get to the top. I knew if I kept working towards health, that I had a chance to heal. If I gave up, or simply berated myself for struggling, then there was no chance at recovery. I had hope and my will to thrive. I was going to work for it.

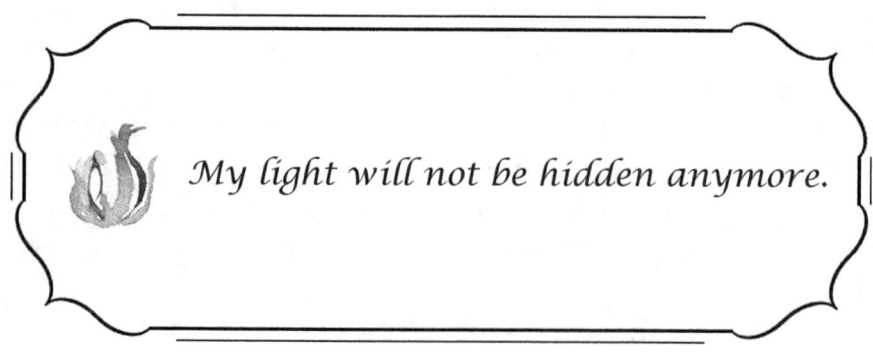

My light will not be hidden anymore.

Celebrate Every Step

The moment I believed that I could make the top of the stairs, I'd already won.

Soul Fire

A month after my mother died, walking up the stairs felt, simply put, insurmountable. Yet, I was stubborn. I was determined to climb those stairs. At my lowest, I could climb three to four stairs at a time before stopping to breathe and rest. It would have been far easier to add meaning to those moments or to let it get me down. At my core, even then I knew that positive thinking was the way out of that moment.

If there were a devil on one shoulder at that moment, he may have said, "You can't do this. Just give up now. You're overweight anyway and did this to yourself. Why do you even bother?" There have been times in my life that I have allowed those negative thoughts into my soul. I have allowed them into my heart. They have held space in my home with my babies. How dare they? How dare I let them take up space in my life?

When I looked up at the dark, seemingly endless carpeted stairs wondering how the heck I'd get to the top, I lived in each moment. Sometimes the moment is one breath; one breath in and then releasing it out. I had to get to the bathroom and it was upstairs. I was only using one bathroom so my family could be exposed to me as little as possible. For my children, I would do anything.

In another lesser moment I may have let that devil speak and hold space in my mind. When it really mattered, I showed up for myself. I immediately held up my hand firmly, said stop in my mind and silenced the negativity. I said to myself, *I'll do what I can do, rest and do it all again.* My mother did that. She climbed those very stairs not so long before. She struggled in silence, holding her heavy, long-haired cat Meg. She climbed, rested, and climbed again. You know what?

Celebrate Every Step

She made it to the top every single time. Her pace may not have been anyone else's. She carried her precious cargo up to her room and made it each time. A month after she took her very last peaceful breath, I said to myself if she could do it, then so can I!

Sometimes, when we share our darkest moments, our most vulnerable times, we feel trampled on. Humans often like to add things to someone else's sharing for their own comfort rather than listen deeply and fully. I've done it many times myself. When you come through a dark moment and step into the light, it's easy to feel naked and on stage for the world to see. Those moments of emergence are so vital and so intimate. It's important to step into the light fully and stand up tall. I allowed myself to feel accomplished when I climbed four stairs instead of three at a time. Who cares if most people climb a flight or two or ten at a time with ease? (Our minds like to exaggerate our disparities if we let them.)

Sharing my journey with COVID has come with feeling very naked and vulnerable. Some people judged the nurses and doctors when I told them what happened. Some people kept digging for why I got it or where, and who exactly was to blame. Some people even blamed me for spending time in the hospital with my mother. Most of those people didn't know me very well. Those who knew me knew that I went through the scientific gauntlet in my mind prior to making any decisions. That one doubting Thomas, that one disbeliever hurt my heart. For a time, I allowed my own doubts to emerge from the depths and take root.

I realized I had allowed that negativity to have space in my soul. I even believed some of the terrible things that it said. Then I came to my senses, held my hand up strong and said "Stop!" The way to win any race, any struggle, any dream is to take action one step and one moment at a time. For me, in 2020, that was literal. Every single morning, I woke up and I was grateful to be able to hug my beautiful children. Every time I see the sunshine, or the rain fall, I am grateful for the experience.

Celebrate every single step in your life. Whether you're dealing with depression, a weight loss struggle, going to college, relationship issues, or a health issue, celebrate each victory. It is absolutely worth it to do so! Sometimes, celebrating and being your own cheerleader is the single thing that helps you go on. If things are hard, remind yourself of all the good in your life. Focus on what you want in your life.

I realize that sometimes it's incredibly hard to see the light through the darkness or the fog. Sometimes getting help from a professional is the vital key to seeing the light again. There's no shame in that. Help can come from many sources. A wise woman once said that it doesn't matter where the therapy comes from, as long as it comes.

Every single day is a gift. Everything in my life has led me to that simple truth. Health is what you make it as well. You may have debilitating things to deal with in this life. Some may call them scars even. Yet, your state of mind vastly impacts how your body and mind feel each day.

The moment I believed that I could make the top of the stairs, I'd already won. I took as deep a breath as I could then and grabbed the railing firmly as I slowly and yet deliberately picked up my foot. The sun began to emerge on that darkened hallway in that instant. I had already reached the top of the stairs in my mind. I simply knew that no matter how long it took me, I would get there. I knew that I would keep trying at my own pace. I squashed each judgement and comparison to my healthy self as it came. I celebrated each step as I climbed it.

When I say this, please know that the stairs changed over time. What I celebrated evolved with me as I gained muscle, endurance, and more health. It took me a month to climb the whole stairs without stopping. Then I channeled my father after his stroke and picked a new goal. Look to your heroes for strength. Most importantly, remember to be your own hero.

Look at the times you are proud of in your life. What made each moment special? Did you overcome the impossible? Did you walk again after a terrible accident, injury, or stroke? Were you the first in your family to graduate high school? What thoughts did you allow in your heart and mind during that time?

If this exercise is hard for you, pretend that you're writing about a stranger. Bear with me for a moment, it works, I promise. You can start with your own heroes if that's helpful. What qualities did they possess in those moments that you're drawn to? Now, find those moments you're proud of in your life. What did you tell yourself in those moments that allowed you to accomplish the task?

I'll go first. In my darkest moments when I thought my stepfather may kill me on any given night, I told myself that I would not give up. I told myself that I would not go easily. When he did everything to make me invisible, I did not cower. He got rid of the phone, moved us forty minutes away, and tried to take me out of my school and dance class. I would not leave the schools. I instinctively knew that if I allowed that to happen, then he would erase me completely. Out of great darkness and pain emerged a survivor. What worked about those moments was the determination. Where there was depression, I forced myself to still engage in the light. I dove deep into dance, sculpture, and writing. I forced myself to talk with people even when I really didn't want to. I wouldn't call myself a hero. I endured complete hell with a very dangerous man in order to graduate high school. I was still one of the lucky ones.

Whether your hurt is big or small, celebrate the moments where you are your own hero. Celebrate making it to the gym, or taking that walk you've promised yourself. Rather than reminding yourself of the months where you didn't get that job done; celebrate your wins. That step you took may seem small to some and also be huge to you. We all have our own unique crosses to bear. You may not always see your neighbors' scars. I believe that love is the answer. My hope is that the pandemic has reminded all of us how vital compassion is to healing.

Compassion may look like being patient and giving yourself grace. It may look like being kind when someone tells you about their experience during the pandemic. It may be as simple as a smile, eye contact, and treating someone with love and respect. We come to the table with different perspectives, experiences, and baggage. We can all feel love. Sometimes it's harder to let in than others. It's all the more important in those moments. When things look and feel the worst, we have the capacity to be our best. Remember to celebrate the mundane tiny victories too. They just may end up being the most important of all.

Celebrate Every Step

When COVID hit, everyone wanted to blame someone or something. The truth is, that there's no one to blame for some situations. Pointing the finger can make someone feel incredibly justified. There were contributing factors to increased loss of life due to rhetoric, for instance. The divisiveness didn't help anyone.

Our brains went to work on the big, hard problems. We wanted to solve them like a jigsaw puzzle. It most likely didn't solve anything though. The scientists in the labs who went to work on finding vaccines helped a great deal. You may firmly disagree on this point. That's okay. Compassion is what will give us all a future with hope.

Everyone asked me, "where do you think you got it from?" I can point to three specific sources of contact. The truth is, that pointing fingers will not fix it or take it away. I don't think the hospital did anything 'wrong' per se. It was disconcerting to overhear that there was at least one confirmed COVID case across the hall from my mother's room. I also know that HIPAA privacy laws put medical professionals in a tough place with this. I know that each provider that cared for Mom did their absolute best not to spread it.

Diseases aren't new. Bacteria and viruses aren't new. We as lay people don't hear about all the things that medical professionals have done to keep us safe. For many years they've been following protocols to keep us all safe. Maybe some weren't as strict before the pandemic. As a former EMT and pre-med student, I know that medical professionals train for this almost subconsciously on a daily basis. They do not want to spread bacteria, or viruses to anyone. They bust their butts every day to save people. Some don't want to be saved. Be willing to see the good in people.

The truth is that in every contact I had with anyone, I did the best I could to keep myself and others healthy. I chose with what information I had at the time. Other than our household, I don't believe we personally infected anyone else, thank God. When I was sick, I stayed home. When I felt better, I followed sound science, CDC guidelines, and full disclosure to anyone I was in contact with. That's what kindness and compassion looked like to me in 2020.

One morning, I felt well enough to drink coffee for the first time in almost a week. I felt frisky and energetic even. Mind you, I was sitting quietly at my dining room table. I felt good and wanted to do something with my energy. So, I began trying to do some family genealogy. How hard could that be? I'd done it before. Old newspapers should have something, right?

From the moment I turned on the computer, I realized that I wasn't all there. It was like I was drunk without alcohol. My mind felt slow and confused, foggy even. It's never a good sign when opening a website causes confusion. I forged ahead anyway, and typed a few words into the search engine, still hopeful. Nothing looked useful. Each box to check may as well have been Egyptian, because I didn't understand what any of them were for. Mind you, I'm not a genealogist. I'm interested in the subject both for my family and historic value. These searches aren't my forte. That's ok, I can learn, right? Not today!

I finally went to the FAQ page of the website to discover what the elusive boxes meant and how to navigate the page. The second I got there; I realized that I wasn't ready for this information. How is it that I could type, semi-cohesively, but I couldn't read and learn new terms? I had no clue. Brain fog did not feel logical at all.

I have had to be okay with the unknown medically at times. As someone who dedicated a decade of my life to medicine and science, that was not easy to do. Most humans, I'd wager, don't sit well with the unknown. They'd prefer to pretend, look away, or rationalize by adding their own spin on things.

For a month I breathed through a straw. For days I wasn't sure if I'd see the sunrise the next day, or hug my children another day, let alone watch them grow. That wasn't just fear talking, it was reality. I honestly was not sure if I'd live another day. I learned from that and other life experience that one moment was what I had.

Healing took more than two years. It took me telling myself repeatedly that things would heal. I kept pushing myself slowly and safely. I kept eating antioxidant foods. I got stronger. It was painfully slow. Improvement was still worth celebrating. There may be residual effects that stay with me. I've learned to cope and change with my body, rather than fighting it.

Celebrating every step is more than just my literal staircase. It's more than healing from COVID. Celebrating every step is giving myself credit for stepping out of my comfort zone that day. It's about acknowledging what I can control. That's honestly not too much. The unknown forces us to see that we aren't able to control everything. I can choose my own actions. I can choose not to berate myself for not being fast enough, or perfect enough. More than that, I can choose to celebrate every step.

As a culture, we tend to celebrate big things. If I had a goal weight for example, I would only be proud of myself for reaching that exact weight. If I lost one pound due to healthy eating and lifestyle, that would go unnoticed. If I was one pound heavier than my goal weight, it would not be meaningful to me with this way of thinking. I might look at the scale, not see what I want and then go eat poorly to punish myself. Losing thirty pounds is a larger accomplishment made of tiny ones we do daily.

Healing from this huge illness was a large undertaking. Within each situation, problem or issue, there were smaller victories. Giving myself permission to celebrate the small ones fueled me to continue. The stairs were climbed one step at a time.

 *Remember to celebrate the mundane tiny victories too. They just may end up being the most important of all.*

"Post" Illness: Living Again

The internal fallacy was that accepting what happened somehow meant accepting defeat. Accepting that gave me the ability to see it did not have to define me.

Vulnerability should be added to the list of four-letter words. Disregard the fact that it doesn't only have four letters. My survivor's brain said that anyway. Those of us who live life as independent strong people don't always know how to be vulnerable. An illness or an accident can render anyone forever changed. For survivors, the need to rely on someone for something doesn't come naturally.

Post illness for me was when I could be out of bed more than I was in bed. There were moments I thought the day would never come. After almost a month in seclusion, I was desperate for human connection. Music, as always provided the doorway to life. That day was positively glorious.

Who knew they'd be releasing *Hamilton* for people to have musicals while at home? Who knew how very important this musical would become to a lot of people for a variety of reasons, including myself?

Stepping outside like a fledgling baby bird, I left my nest. The day was warm, with a deep blue sky and tiny fluffy white clouds. Stepping outside for the first time in weeks, the sun made me blink and cringe back. I closed my eyes, held my head high, and let the sun lap my face like the first bath of a brand-new baby. The weeds were piling up in the yard. I could do that one flower bed, I told myself, desperate to do anything except lie in the bed. Panting, I grabbed the tan and green plastic seat on wheels and sat down carefully.

I've never been so grateful for my aunt's gift of the rolling garden seat in all my life. She'd given it to me when she sold her house and moved into an apartment. I gracefully accepted it and stored my garden tools in the space provided under the hard plastic lid. That day, more than any other though, I

"Post" Illness: Living Again

really needed that seat. I straightened up my back, grateful to be above the dirt and began to weed.

It was then that I heard "Wait for It" from *Hamilton*. Several different friends and family had recommended the play to me. My arms and legs were sluggish from disuse. My brain was foggy, as if I'd just woken in the middle of the night. I'd been told about the unique combination of rap and Broadway music. Intrigued, I downloaded it that morning to give it a go. The fast rhythm began. I breathed in deeply and listened. Each verse spoke to me, as if Lin Manuel Miranda knew my struggle in that exact moment.

I was a person who got things done. I had fought to survive unimaginable terror. I was a military spouse and a mom. I was the president of a school volunteer organization. Currently, I was also quite unwell. That did not sit well with me. Worlds collided as my independence met the reality of my current health struggle. The situation felt unfair. The waiting to climb the proverbial stairs felt endless. I was a go-getter who got things done. At that moment, I could barely step outside my back porch without passing out. I found hope in the words "Wait For It."

I unearthed my phlox and liriope while listening to the passions of Burr and Hamilton. Feeling so far behind the eight ball; I chose to do what I could in each moment. Reframing was necessary for me. I had to look at my life as it actually was in that moment, rather than who I knew myself to be. I didn't have to give up hope. I needed to accept what I could not change. I got my butt kicked by COVID. The internal fallacy was that accepting what happened somehow meant accepting defeat. Accepting that gave me the ability to see that it did not have to define me.

Viewing weeding as strength training would have seemed preposterous until that moment. When I heard that song, I realized that I was at a temporary rest stop. I may not have known where I would end up, but I didn't have to stop trying in each moment to regain my life. Deep down, that was also a metaphor for my inner journey of survival.

Patience has never been my strong suit. It's also the biggest lesson of my life. There have been multiple times when I had to shift my focus from wanting to run like a cheetah to waiting with purpose. That day in the garden, I did not run. I did not look like I was running a marathon. I was though, bit by bit and weed by weed. Sometimes our best lessons are learned in the waiting. Waiting did not have to mean giving up or giving in.

Deep inside all of us there is a life force full of passion and drive. It's the still small voice inside of you that wants to stand up and give your gifts to the world. It's an inner knowing that comes before and completely separate of inner doubting. That day in the garden, the sun shone washing hope over me. I could see then that I was going to live. I began to believe that I could recover.

COVID is a wildcard. You have no clue what you're going to get. My son had the sniffles and a light cough for a couple days. My daughter was much the same with a fever for one day. I was in bed for a month with low eighty percent oxygenation in my blood, and throat so swollen I literally didn't know if it would swell shut each day for a month. So, what does life look like after COVID's acute phase? It was completely different for myself than it was for my family. In a way, I'm really grateful that they didn't suffer. I'm grateful to be such a fighter with a strong will to live. My family are survivors

"Post" Illness: Living Again

too, but as their mom and wife, I'm grateful not to have to put their fortitude to the test. They've been through enough, all of them.

The fall season for me means planting things that sometimes need the winter to process and then bloom in the spring. More recently, I've also begun planting pansies in the fall. Having grown up in the north, that thought seemed preposterous. In New York state, you plant pansies in the spring and they die in the fall. Down here in Virginia though, they're on the opposite timeline. You plant them in the fall and reap the benefits of flowers all winter until the summer heat comes full force, around Mother's Day.

I signed up to go plant picking with the garden club the beginning of October of 2020. This meant I got to go to the nursery, see all the beautiful plants, and help select the healthiest of the bunch for our socially distanced plant sale. I thought I was 'better'. I knew I'd get tired. What I didn't realize was that my body would tell me exactly what it was willing to give and no more.

We'd been there for several hours picking white, purple, yellow, maroon pansies and gorgeous fall mums of all shapes and sizes. It was bliss being outside in the nursery and with friends, regardless of the mask. We'd been there for five hours before I realized it. Suddenly, I saw black spots in my vision and hit an energy wall that I could no longer push past. I had to do the very basic head between my legs maneuver to keep from passing out right there next to the flowers. My back screamed from being unused for so long. Stretching I could deal with. It made me happy to have 'normal' soreness from a workout, no matter how humble it was. For certain, it was humbling being in the presence of people ten, twenty and thirty years older than myself who were in much better shape. I could not dwell here though. This is what's so, I told myself. It too shall pass. It was temporary.

We were able to have a safe sale out in the driveway and I'd purchased some white pansies. Mom loved pansies and the white is visible from the road, cheering people up all winter. Some mums that were several years old in pots were blooming in the back yard. *They'd look nice up front by the walkway,* I thought.

That morning I woke with a lot of thick mucus and congestion in my lungs, like I'd had daily during the acute phase of the illness. Exercise could work through that and help clear it, I thought. So, during Mom's birthday week in mid-October I thought I'd plant them. The eight-inch clay pots were so heavy I almost passed out carrying them forty feet to the front of the house. Bear in mind that I used to regularly carry eighty-pound wheels of Parmigiano Reggiano when I worked at a cheese shop years ago. More recently, I was an EMT, lifting patients and for years I'd been a military spouse. Talk about humbling. *It's ok,* I told myself again. *It too will pass.*

What people didn't know at first was that you didn't just get over COVID if you were in my category. For us, getting over COVID was like getting over a stroke. We worked harder for the simplest things, appreciated them more, and got exhausted by tying our shoes or weeding the yard. We got tired in the same way as a person recovering from a stroke, or maybe even more. There were those long haulers that had trouble doing the simplest things and breathing at the same time.

When you've had a stroke and survive, your body works so hard to do things like chew, talk, and walk. It's exhausting business. There is something innately

"Post" Illness: Living Again

similar about this recovery process. It remains to be seen how much I will 'get over' COVID. I know that I will do my part to heal. Each day will push myself harder, longer, and farther, within reason. When my body says it needs to rest, I will give it rest. When I do, my muscles get stronger and I can breathe better. My heartrate isn't as high for as long.

The exercise scientist in me felt terribly degraded. I was the woman who watched her father and husband both survive and recover from multiple strokes who chose to rise to this unique challenge. I could only accomplish what my mind believed I could. If I defeated myself at the starting block of my healing, I stunted my recovery. Choosing was half the battle. I chose to recover.

For a while, simple days with low-level activity left me bone tired like my husband post-strokes. Sometimes, it was just a normal day and he was stressed. Others, he was falling asleep early because he pulled weeds in the yard with me. A thought occurred to me after waking from a deep-sleep nap that once again happened far too early in the night. *Maybe I should be working myself as hard as a stroke survivor does in their Physical and Occupational Therapy.* My journey was not the same as my husband's. My journey was uniquely my own. Yet the similarities were uncanny.

Listening to my body kept me alive. It helped me recover. It helped me to rebuild my body in the aftermath.

What it meant to work hard physically was at least temporarily altered for me. There were a couple days that my physical therapy was making candles in the kitchen and chocolate cups filled with chocolate mousse.

Soul Fire

Being unstoppable is a secret superpower of a survivor. When the world thinks we can't do X, then we do just that. That particular day, I was exhausted. In this case, I didn't think I had anything in me, except a long nap. My children, however, were eager to learn creatives. For them, I would have moved mountains. As fate would have it, a friend gave me some beautiful candle wax. I inherited candle making supplies from my aunt, my mother, and had some of my own. I couldn't let good candle wax or fun go to waste. Heck, my kitchen island was still filled with my carrot harvest from the garden. My mom had planted those carrots.

A plan was hatched, and the joy of that moment spread like wildfire. This particular choice was unstoppable because my kitchen was already messy, and the wax pot was huge. Candle-making could leave wax everywhere. The choice was easy to create, however. I created candles from the shavings. I created the joy where it was needed. I fed the love from the friend's gift, the creativity, and small scientists' minds. We made candles.

Before we began, we had to cut the carrots to prepare them to freeze until we could use them. Next, we had to excavate the gear from the depths of the garage. Climbing around a half-built jewelry box, my mother's beloved books we had yet to find the perfect homes for, and our own accumulated stuff. We unearthed the candles-only crockpot, molds, scents, and wicks. When we moved her things into the house after she passed, I didn't have the heart to sort the candle gear. I remembered each and every purchase she made. I remember that Mom bought this wick and these dyes in that tiny store on vacation that year. I was half her height then and maybe seven years old.

"Post" Illness: Living Again

These very old scents and each piece represented the beauty of that innocence and the completeness of the love. I still was happy to get rid of the old, spoiled scents and pieces that would no longer serve anyone. I reminded myself that I still got to keep the memories, turned the other way and threw the old in the trash can.

Taking a moment to feel the emotions, process, and to be honest with myself was vital to grief and any recovery. I chose each time I passed an undone thing on the to-do list. That particular day, I chose to organize the candle supplies, use some useful items, and create Christmas gifts from scraps that were in someone's garage for who knows how long. The best part was that the children got to witness that process for the first time. It was poetic in a way, completing the circle. Dealing with things as they came into the path helped me not to be overwhelmed. That year especially there were so very many things that could possibly overwhelm me. It felt like less of a choice and more of a moral imperative to process, sort, and still create joy daily.

We honored both of my parents like a two for one birthday almost. Dad loved chocolate and Mom loved making candles. To be more accurate, Mom had a childlike joy when we would happen upon a candle making store in the middle of nowhere on our summer vacations. Inevitably we'd have to stop so she could find the rare treasures she called tools of her craft. Dad similarly spoke of his vacation in Columbia or Peru when they placed 'really fine chocolates' on his pillows each day at the hotel. He came home from that trip a reawakened man. He no longer abstained from the pure joy of chocolate. He found a way to moderation in all things and only brought in the house what he was willing to eat. He recognized his limitations and planned accordingly. We chose to honor them with joy. The chocolate and candles would hopefully be a happy memory in my children's eyes. They took part, made decisions, and helped where they could. I even got brave and allowed them to break up the bigger bricks of wax with the knife once we'd used the shavings from the pot. No one was maimed. No blood was spilled. We did make nineteen candles though.

I became unstoppable for my babies. I became unstoppable for my own emotional well-being. Healing from illness took time and patience I didn't have before the incident. I had to be patient with myself where I was each day. I had to listen to my body, rather than ignore every ache, pain, and body signal. I had trained myself as a dancer to push through the normal body aches, blistered feet, and hunger pangs.

This was brand new territory. I had to listen hard to each body signal, healthy food craving, and cry for rest. Listening to myself, giving my body credit for knowing what it needed was vital to healing in the unknown territory. Once I realized that I was still alive, I got to work on living again.

Vulnerability didn't have to be the bad guy. I wasn't less of a person because my body had changed. I was in fact more empathetic and sympathetic with those who experienced physical and mental disabilities. I didn't have to like where I was mentally and physically. Liking it had nothing to do with accepting it. My body was different post illness. I could improve my overall health. Both were true.

"Post" Illness: Living Again

 *Vulnerability didn't have to be the bad guy. I wasn't less of a person because my body had changed. My body was different post illness. I could improve my overall health. Both were true.*

Soul Fire

Grief Isn't a Competition

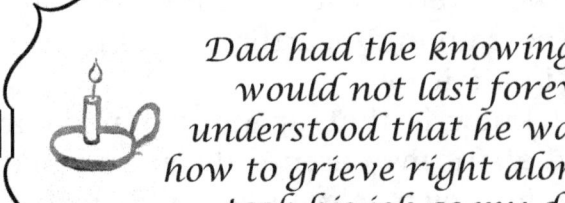

Dad had the knowing that sadness would not last forever. He also understood that he was teaching me how to grieve right along with him. He took his job as my dad seriously.

Grief comes in many forms or facets and often without warning. Growing up, I was fortunate not to be touched by death or loss until I was a teenager. I had a childhood insulated with love and not a small measure of luck. I don't remember a time before I knew about grief. My parents divorced when I was eleven. That was my first experience with loss. I went through it alone, it felt like. I didn't understand why my chest ached, or how anyone could feel so terrible. It was foreign. I didn't understand deep loss until it came to my doorstep. Then it mattered. Thankfully, my dad was there to help.

When I was fourteen years old, my father taught me about grief for what felt like the first time. Dad picked me up in his gold station wagon every other Friday to go back with him for weekend visits. That particular weekend Dad picked me up, I was devastated. My first real boyfriend had moved to South Carolina and we'd broken up. Dad, as life had it, also had broken up with his first girlfriend since my mother. When we saw each other as I opened the door to his car that evening, we understood what we were each going through instinctively. I read the pain and heartbreak in his eyes as clearly as looking in a mirror.

What some didn't know is that up until that point I'd made up my mind about my parents' divorce and I'd decided, based on my own eleven-year-old expert opinion, that it was all my father's fault. I'd stayed up late into the nights listening to their fights beginning at seven years old. Having only heard him, it must've been his fault. What I could not know about those arguments and their marriage would fill another book. I later learned that they couldn't see eye to eye with each other back then. He got sober, went to counselling, and

Grief Isn't a Competition

really craved personal growth. She wanted to stay in her shell, safe, sound, and hiding. That didn't work out too well. They began walking different paths.

That night when Dad picked me up, my chilly this-is-your-fault heart began to soften. Truthfully, it all melted away on that hour long drive. Dad was always honest with me. His sad eyes teared up as we listened to love songs.

"What's wrong, Dad?" I asked. My heart had already seen that look in his eyes that resonated with how I felt.

"My girlfriend left me this week. I'm just a bit sad. This is what grief looks like," he said.

Dad let the tears fall down his cheeks. He didn't bother to wipe them away. He wasn't ashamed to feel things. He appreciated beauty in music, movies, literature, and people. He was sad to lose the beauty in the relationship. He was grateful for what he'd learned with her. He had the knowing that sadness would not last forever. He also understood that he was teaching me how to feel right along with him. He took his job as my dad seriously.

He started that night sharing what grief was, what it looked like and how to deal with it. "I figure, since I'm learning about grief, I may as well teach you what I'm learning," he said earnestly. "You deserve to have all the tools for success and grief is a big one. Now, please pull out a tape and put it in the tape deck for me," Dad said.

The grief group, weekly meetings with his psychologist, and AA each gave him different tools. From that night on, Dad and I were dealing with our breakups together. We were united there, and had a place of belonging, even if we desperately didn't want to belong to that group. We weren't alone.

"Grief isn't a competition, Sweet Baby, no matter what some may say. We are both on the journey together and yet still walking our own paths," Dad said a little choked up. "Each of us wants to find that one we can trust with our hearts forever. She said I wasn't her one. That cuts me to the quick. But, day by day we will feel those feelings and be able to move on," he said. "We have to acknowledge them first and welcome the feelings like old friends in order to say goodbye to them."

Dad always knew exactly what to say to make me feel better. It wasn't a magic fix it button. In those moments, he heard my heart, listened, and let me know that I wasn't alone. He stood beside me to listen to the hurt of the loss of that love, and others throughout the years. Until his last breath, my father loved me. I'll go out on a limb and say that love never dies. One of his best phrases was, "There's never enough time with those we love." When my mother was dying, I told her that I amended his statement to: "There's never enough time with those we love, and that love never dies."

For six months or so Dad and I took turns listening, singing songs in the car, and talking about the weeks in between our visits. At fourteen, I'd begun to understand the world differently.

We used music to soothe our inner savage beasts. My dad was a musician among other things. He played air piano as an emotional release as he drove down the road. He talked about the parts of the song, especially if they caught his attention. He talked about the lyrics, melody, and chords and how they made him feel. On the one hand, I learned some music theory. On the other, I began to see music as cathartic. We saw ourselves in the songs. We felt the feelings, released them into the air to eventually let them go. The music helped us to heal ourselves.

By the time Christmas came that year, any self-righteous knowing I had about fault or blame in their divorce had washed away. I realized that the truth of their divorce was far more complex, there were two sides to every story and the truth somewhere in between. I also realized that I didn't have to assign blame to one of them even if their pain asked me to do just that. I could love both my parents for who they were with me, regardless of their marital status. Love and listening got Dad and I through the divorce and the break-ups. They would get us through many, many things throughout the rest of his life as well.

Birthdays and anniversaries bring up grief like clockwork. Dad's birthday is no different. For the first time since he died, my children wanted to celebrate his birthday with joy. The pain of losing him is less and what remains is their love for him and his for them. We made chocolate cupcakes. Love does not die when our loved ones pass on. They may take their last breaths in any number of ways, but love lives forever. When your young children want to celebrate a birthday, you want to celebrate with them. When it's your beloved father and he happens to be deceased, you celebrate creatively.

Grief and the stages therein are expressions of love that is much changed and is usually an unwanted change. Sometimes grief is the time when we're able to process old hurts, or unresolved issues. Some of us are challenged to deal with it at all and remain in an unpleasant stage of grief, like anger forever. My father taught me about grief in real time. We happened to both be experiencing it. I understood that the ache in my chest and even the anger I felt around my parents' divorce was grief.

Some may look at seeking help or support groups as a weakness. What I saw with my father, was a man who was willing to admit his shortcomings and one who chose to overcome each of them as much as he possibly could. Similarly, I chose to follow in his footsteps and walk through the stages. I chose to feel each emotion and to relish in each victory, no matter how small.

Whenever I tell people that my mom passed away, they apologize. It's amazing how one's passing and our frame of mind around that passing can change everything about our grief process. With my dad I was angry, and it felt like nobody said they were sorry. Lots of people have Daddy issues, I guess. I am forever a Daddy's girl. Now that my mom is passed as well; it's very odd for me to feel so differently this time. I love her dearly and I think of her every day. I guess somewhere between a global pandemic, lung cancer, brain cancer, and COVID, my gratitude muscle got a really big workout.

Our country doesn't teach people about grief as a standard rule. Religions teach various things on the matter, of course. In other countries, there are ceremonies of reflection and mourning every month for years when a loved one dies. They wear certain colors to let people know that they mourn. Around the world, different variations on these things exist. Here we usually throw a rug over the pain, sadness, and anger.

Grief Isn't a Competition

Those who have walked the path reach out with the understanding that they have in order to comfort us.

Grief really isn't a competition. It's the pause and reflect button that no one asks to receive. When my parents divorced and later when my first boyfriend and I broke up, I was sad. I was young and didn't understand what was even happening at first. I felt at the mercy of the waves without knowing how to swim.

I felt immense gratitude for my father that day in the station wagon. He got me. He understood pain like mine. He opened the doorway to music, writing, and talking as outlets for the big feelings. He gave me tools in the days that followed for getting through really tough moments. He showed me that it's ok to take care of yourself, even and especially when you're hurting. He taught me that grief has its own timetable and invisible on buttons. He taught me that grief was love and learning wrapped into one.

Grief really isn't a competition. It's the pause and reflect button that no one asks to receive.

Soul Fire

Am I an Orphan or an Elder?

Some of us learned young to be reliable, trustworthy, and to make the best decisions for the group. Before my parents began healing themselves, I was on my own.

Sometimes I'm so very present to the fact that both my parents are dead. They're not passed on, passed out, or deceased. They are dead. It feels as hard and harsh as it sounds, and coldly cuts me to my core. Inevitably, when I reach out with those feelings to someone, I feel like my hand gets slapped. It's an unspoken "just deal with it" I feel when the lines go silent. It isn't anyone's fault that I have strong feelings that day. The emotions are mine to deal with and the absolute nature of that is deafening.

Sitting with the truth, my truth, is indeed mine to do. It's no one's job to fix me. The experience I had in 2020 is that old story, *I'm on my own.* My inner child grumbles and says, *of course I'm on my own.* It's almost as if not having a mother or father alive who makes themselves available to me is so much bigger when I feel grief. I would've called Dad as a teenager, bared my soul, and gotten off the phone with a solution and a sense of being held in the golden light of his townhouse on the hill. When he moved in with us, I just knocked on his door and vented in much the same way. In the last five years I had Mom, I also leaned on her to vent, chat, or sort out the big things there were to deal with. That is, when I wasn't pretending to be impervious to pain, I allowed myself to lean on her.

Now when I feel big feelings, there's no one to take them to. My aching lonely heart says, *they're dead remember?* The slap in the face keeps coming at those times.

Don't get me wrong; there are people who love me. Those same people have also been dealing with pandemic level inquiries and stressors of their own. I get that it's going to be okay. The storms will pass.

Am I an Orphan or an Elder

Still, I'm left with the query in my war-torn heart. Am I an orphan or just the elder in the family now?

I could be big and bold and brave when I felt capable before. Dad always treated me like a reasonable rational human, unless OCD got in his way. My parents both always made time for me and dropped everything to just be with whatever I had going on in any given moment.

The grief from the lack of their physical presence is felt so strongly in the moments where I feel small. When I have no elder who will drop everything and be there reliably for me, the hole of the loss of those who had that place is even more glaring. The black hole mocks me even as I just want to be curled up under a blanket watching mindless television to comfort myself.

My father would say that was addictive behavior. The urge to run from big huge things can be strong sometimes. Being willing to plant my feet and be the adult in the room is always a good character-building exercise. I'm learning that when the buck stops with me, I always have to be the adult, the strong one. That way of thinking is a fallacy. Regardless, it feels so real when the emotions are overwhelming. Everyone else has their own big things they have to deal with in their lives. It's not true that I don't matter. The lonely little girl inside of me who mourns her parents feels that way sometimes.

I've learned that it's important to be honest with myself about my feelings. That's especially true if the emotions are huge. Creating space to breathe is a vital part of my resiliency. Sometimes that means a blanket and mindless television. If I don't get them out in some form, even a journal, the emotions threaten my peace long term. I'm thankful for those vessels of peace. It's important that I'm honest with myself. It isn't always sunshine and roses. As a friend said recently, there are thorns on the roses. It's our job to remember to smell the roses and to remember how soft and lovely the blooms are as well. Sometimes we feel the thorns. We don't need to make a crown of them or completely lose ourselves in the sharp thorny briars.

One moment of connection with another soul can make us feel the sun on our perfect petal cheeks. True happiness comes from deep inside, not from what others give to us. Sometimes we all need even a tiny gentle reminder that the sun is shining. The truth is that I am both orphan and elder now. My parents loved me dearly. I never question that truth. Sometimes that sacred space they held open for me, whenever I needed it, bleeds a little. The wound of their passing is felt sharply like the thorn sometimes. It's because the love was so good and so sweet that the missing is that much larger.

Every year, when the fall leaves make their final hurrah of spectacular colors in the Adirondack foothills, I feel the deep pull of New York state. October is a time of change for so many reasons. It's far beyond the fall season. I especially liked visiting home and Mom near her birthday.

There was a time when it was not possible to go to visit safely, but I was very present to that deep feeling that *I should be up North.* In the twenty years I've lived in the south, I've gone up during the fall, all but one year. It was sad on a level that I couldn't express. Every year during the fall I travelled there, hiked the gorges, and photographed the fall beauty. I have always found nature to be so very cathartic.

Am I an Orphan or an Elder

Grieving came in waves. That year, the sadness that I couldn't go home hit me deeply. Borders between states had been closed. Mom was gone and she was celebrating with those who have gone before her. We were here, missing her. I decided to **do** something with that deep sadness.

At Wegmans, I purchased a gallon of apple cider. Usually, I would be picking up fresh cider at a local cider mill. Some in our group would get fresh doughnuts to enjoy with the cider.

It was time to make doughnuts. I couldn't go to New York. Instead, I would bring New York to our home. After breakfast we began peeling the mountain of honey crisp apples. Start to finish; it was more than a twelve-hour process for three types of doughnuts. Apple fritters, lemon curd filled, and raspberry cherry filling, oh my!

When the grief of a season or a date hit me like a ton of bricks, I made doughnuts. I brought New York to me when I couldn't go there myself. Honoring the emotions with grace brought me freedom.

It doesn't matter how many older family members you still have living. If the buck stops with you, then it does. If you're the one that everyone leans on, then you are that one. Some of us learned young to be reliable, trustworthy, and to make the best decisions for the group. Before my parents began healing themselves, I was on my own.

I could've been orphan and elder long before my parents died. I would have been exactly that if I had been unwilling to walk through the journey of forgiveness and inner work. It would've been easier to cut people out of my life than to look at things and try to heal. It would've been easier to do just that in fact. One day, I was ready to step out of my past and I did.

Being responsible is also a function of being a survivor. Survivors are both alone as a concept and often the ones who get it all done. Others often are happy to relinquish the responsibility to us. I have felt alone since I was seven years old even though I had a family who loved me. There were breaks in trust, absolutely. I took on the role of a responsible adult from a very young age.

Now, I realize that I am in fact a woman whose parents have died. I am an orphan in that way. I am also immensely loved and able to feel that love. I have been the one to care for my parents and am now one of the elders in the family.

It doesn't matter how long ago they died or if they died. Being an orphan and an elder could make one feel even more alone in the world. It doesn't have to take on that meaning, however. I could choose to view my place in the family as one of honor. I could see that while they are gone, they were here. They taught me how to love, to take care of things, and how to be the one other people look to for answers.

I'm the one who teaches myself how to feel the love. Letting love in starts at home, with me. If love never dies, then there is also an honoring of the elders who came before me when I feel and pass on that love.

May you have those in your life who have you feel less alone. May you find your people if you haven't found them in your blood. May you make peace with all of it. May you always be able to find the blossoms through the thorns. May you have your person who will drop everything for you at any time to just hear your heart's fire. May you have the strength to start fresh

Am I an Orphan or an Elder

again the next day even if you have to lick your wounds at times. Human beings are blissfully full of well-rounded emotions. We have pain, pleasure, sadness, happiness, and love all in one package. May you feel less alone in the world and more connected to every fiber of the intricately woven spider web of your life. May love find you safely cradled in your sacred safe place.

When you're walking through the fire; may you have the strength to endure with grace. We can only be in one day at a time. There may be a million things on the to do list. We can only do one at a time. That's all we were meant to do.

I could've been orphan and elder long before my parents died. I would have been exactly that if I had been unwilling to walk through the journey of forgiveness and inner work. It would've been easier to cut people out of my life than to look at things and try to heal.

Soul Fire

I Danced Today: Staying Alive

I realized that I could still live a full life after what happened. It might not be the same as it was beforehand. But I could live.

Dance combined two things I loved, music and movement. I wanted to be a professional dancer once upon a time. Moving the emotions through my body helped me understand myself as I grew up. The music may have been celebratory, sad, or full of love. When I danced, I felt free. I felt seen. I felt heard. The beautiful wooden floors held me up. The mirror echoed the outward display of feelings too scary to express.

I had no idea if I would ever be able to dance again after getting COVID. For eight months I counted myself lucky to be breathing air with other living humans and to be healing day by day. Every morning I woke up to see my children's faces and every night I put them to bed I counted myself lucky. For most of those eight months I thought it could be too much to ask to be able to go back to a "normal" life. I had to simply be in each moment. I couldn't make it mean anything that I had to take a nap to get through the day. Blaming myself, or something else, would not have helped me heal. It would have kept me angry.

Every day was different from the moment I felt ill that first time. If I took each day as it came, then I was able to be grateful for every victory, no matter how small. I couldn't allow the doubt or the fear of being a failure as a mom or a wife consume me. Those thoughts only lead down the path of death whether physical or emotional. I had come too close to death for my liking already. I chose life.

I could not possibly have done dance class one day earlier. The very real flip side of that coin is that I could not possibly have waited one more day to begin going to dance class. The week before I think I actually felt my muscles wasting away. My calves had a weird tingling and micro-movement feeling. *That's it!* I shouted in my mind. *I will not wait any longer. I need my life back!*

I went down the mental checklist in the blink of an eye, sitting there surrounded by scrapbook materials. I felt like a caged tiger engulfed in a sea of papers, stickers, and scrapbooks. It's true I may be an animal who had to be patient and allow my body to heal. Conversely, like the rehabilitated tiger who instinctively knows when they are capable of running again, I knew I could.

Just to be sure, I asked myself the scientific questions. Had my heart been beating oddly? No, I'd only felt that once a month or so. In the beginning it was all the time but now my heart seemed to be in check. Could I walk without blacking out? Yes, my outdoor walks and trips to the store had given me some stamina. Had I blacked out lately? No, it had been a while since that happened.

The worst time I saw black spots was when Jen made me laugh. I'd been driving the van with Jen. She and I have been close for fifteen years, since the Diner Days. Jen and her husband Dennis have become family. In the van that day she said something very small and we shared an inside joke at the flooded-back-memories. I laughed. It was a simple thing, you would think. The truth is that I do not remember the last time I laughed like that. I hadn't laughed very much since March of 2020. It was both a scary moment being the driver at the time and a big deal. Sometimes, I had to take the wins with the losses. I was very grateful that nothing serious happened that day.

I definitely still got winded walking up the stairs. I didn't have any episodes walking ten feet to the bathroom anymore though. Going through in my mind what I learned in my exercise science for diseased populations class felt good. I knew some answers. That was great! In that second, I asked myself if I could tolerate aerobics again. The answer was clear. Yes!

I cried as I completed the first dance class since getting COVID. I had to stop a couple times for a few seconds. I only barely started to black out three times as the room closed in on me. It may sound funny to some people, but to me that was a win. When I stopped moving for a few seconds, it got better. Success! I was grateful. Tears of absolute bliss welled in my eyes as we started the cooldown song. I felt very much alive! There's so much magic in **life**.

Whenever anything hard has happened, I found it helped me to count my blessings and deliberately search for the good. The first week in class I had absolutely zero energy reserves. My muscle mass was at an all-time low. My body had a really difficult time maintaining basic levels of oxygen. It would've been very easy to feel defeated. It would've been easy to look around that room full of people that were ten or twenty years older than me and compare myself to them. The truth was the only thing that I needed to compare myself to was my own yesterday.

What was yesterday like for me? Did I do a little more today than yesterday? Back in the early days of recovery, the question was whether or not I stayed awake all day yesterday. My body required a lot of sleep. When I felt ready, I challenged myself to stay awake all day. After reading several peer reviewed journals, I realized that taking a B complex might help me. I talked with my doctor about it and had bloodwork done. My B was low as well as my iron. My body woke up again in stages.

I Danced Today: Staying Alive

My body took the time it took to heal. That process was completely unique to me. My family barely had a blip of a cold when they got it, but they hadn't had recurrent pneumonia as children either.

I worked very, very hard for that next step. The flight of stairs seemed endless. With every step I climbed, I realized I was getting stronger. Progress is progress when you're healing from something.

In those moments of forced patience, I have found myself on a roller coaster of emotions. I'm sure my dad felt much the same when he had his massive stroke and could not walk or even talk properly. Out of sheer willpower and an endless set of stairs; he climbed his way out. He climbed those stairs so much, so well, and so thoroughly that he walked me down the aisle and spoke quite well for the rest of his days.

As I finished that first class, I was reminded of how vital dance has always been in my life. I had a deep connection with the movement of my body and the releasing of emotions. As a dancer, I believed in expressing myself through movement. As a teenager going through trauma with a terrifying stepfather, dance helped save me.

You hear about things like exercise is really important to your health and well-being. As an exercise scientist I learned all the different microcosms of this truth. What I'm speaking about here is a very different type of vitality. It's true that my heart and all of my muscles get a workout every time I step onto that floor. It is also true that I feel the most alive and connected with my life force on the dance floor.

I fuel my Soul Fire when I do what lights me up inside. It's a deep connection with myself. The music flows through me and my emotions are released through the art of dancing.

It's an interesting dichotomy to not want people to stare at me and to also have a deep need to express myself through dance. Let that one sink in for a little bit. When I did not know if Nightmare Man would kill me in my sleep, I showed up to dance. I showed up to the art studio. These two places were my safe havens, my sanctuaries. Not only did I physically and emotionally feel safe inside of the studios. I was also able to say things with my body, my hands and clay that I could not say out loud at the time.

I could not utter the words that I was scared all the way to my core. I could not bring myself to discuss the things I'd been through. But my body could speak. The clay could speak volumes. It may seem smaller and not good enough to some people. For me, it was my saving grace. No matter what hard time I've gone through, I have leaned into my safe places and my outlets. Dance and sculpting were physical movements and representations of my emotions. The huge, complicated lava had a place to go to be released. Through my body movements, I was able to lessen some of the molten hot volcano that boiled under the surface.

When I got COVID in 2020, I literally fought for my life. I felt crippled and disabled in the aftermath. I felt like I'd lost my limbs in an invisible war. Going back felt like getting a prosthetic leg. It felt like I had my life back. It was different. It wasn't easy. It was beautiful though. It was mine.

Some days my body was still so tired you would think I hadn't slept in weeks. When my monthly cycle came it was like that for a solid week. That's a post illness change. For some reason, the third time I went back to working out I found myself lacking motivation. It'd been raining for days here. Seventy-five percent of

I Danced Today: Staying Alive

the country was getting snow which was quite uncommon. Texas had record-breaking power outages and snow that didn't come from a machine.

It was one of those days that you could stay in the covers warm and cuddly all day. Add that typical rainy day feeling to unexplainable exhaustion for what feels like the millionth day. It would've been easier not to go to the gym. Those were the moments for me that made or broke my routine. What I chose to do in those moments helped to change my default (or not). I got up and put my dancing shoes on and went to dance class. I was so glad I did.

The gleam in my eyes sparkled as I turned to my husband later and told him: "I danced today." I was proud of myself, sure. More than that though, I realized that I could still live a full life after what happened. It might not be the same as it was beforehand. But I could live.

I did not dance just one day. I went back home to the dance studio. I opened a door that I thought could be forever closed. Every week I gained more muscle and more strength back. I gained more confidence as I was capable of more. Each time got a little easier. The phenomenal part of dance class is that it worked out my mind, brain, and heart muscle all at once. Once that door was opened, I intended to continue walking in again and again to dance and to be free.

Maybe dancing stresses you out. Perhaps, you like running or even nature hikes. Regardless of how it shows up, do more of what presences that freedom and joy for you. It seems simple. Maybe it seems too simple.

We often make excuses for why we can't take care of ourselves each day. We may say them out loud even. It's quite normal in our culture to ignore our needs until they scream their heads off. Giving myself permission for self-care is not selfish. Self-care presences all the good in my life. It helps me come back to center emotionally. Centering myself with meditation, exercise, hobbies, or even a nap can be life altering. Our bodies and minds tell us what we need. We feel like we need permission from someone else to listen. We only need to give ourselves permission.

Sometimes resting and giving myself grace to have a low key day is what's warranted. The silver lining in this case was that the pace of life was slower when I most needed to slow down. That made resting and decompressing easier.

I've always been my biggest enemy in the resting arena. Often, it felt like there should be some action to take every day. The joke of that is that resting of itself **was** an action. It's often overlooked, underappreciated, and frowned upon. For recovery to be possible, rest was exactly what I needed. Our bodies repair themselves with rest periods between action, specifically during sleep.

Dancing helped me feel alive. What does it mean to stay alive? It's meant different things at different times in my life. It's not a joke or just a song for me. It meant not giving up when I saw no hope.

Staying alive has a much deeper meaning too, as Mr. Godsend explains so well. Some people are "present in the body and absent in the mind," he says. "Some people see differently, like us." He means artists, who see past skin color, past the mediocrity of life, and past the superficial. Artists see and feel deeply. My beautiful children are artists. They are many other things, but they see and feel intensely and deeply. I pray I live long enough to teach them that feelings are great, amazing

I Danced Today: Staying Alive

things that move our souls. May they both know their true callings in this lifetime and know that their parents love them and support them with all their hearts.

We dim our light and lessen our aliveness in many ways. Maybe, like me, you've kept your actions less than your potential knows you can accomplish. Maybe you've sacrificed your passion to accommodate another's dream, or to follow what your parents wanted you to do. Maybe your upbringing was rough like some people near and dear to me. There are times when we each want more from our lives.

Whether Thoreau's words or Shakespeare's speak to you more, whether you're a Democrat, Republican, or Libertarian, whether you're American, Indian, Asian, or Greek, or part of some other group entirely, I welcome you. I welcome you as part of the Us, the We, humanity. These days, we all see, to varying degrees, that the whole world is connected. Our take on that We may be different. I pose that this We, this Us way of thinking is one way we stay alive. We may be the best humans we can be by seeing that our similarities are larger than our differences.

Staying alive has many meanings. It could be literal or metaphorical. It often goes unseen. Aliveness is more than sucking in air. Staying alive is vitality. Give yourself permission to not just survive, or even to just recover. Staying alive is feeding your Soul Fire and choosing to live. Give yourself permission to feel it all and to stay **alive!**

Soul Fire

 *We dim our light and lessen our aliveness in many ways. There are times when we each want more from our lives.*

Overcoming

The fallacy in overcoming adversity is that there's a magic button that you can push, or a secret potion to mend the fabric into a perfect whole shape.

Overcoming anything is a delicate balance of processing, grief work, creating joy, and love. My overcoming has taken on several forms so far. It will take many more before my life's journey is complete.

Underneath it all, I've always known that I had to share my story. The truth shall set you free is a real thing. Honest. To. Goodness. It's more than that though. When I was so ill with COVID that I didn't know if I'd see the next sunrise, I was crystal clear. I'd had enough of God's two-by-four therapy. I had hidden long enough and would hide no more. I would complete what there was to complete and live my life.

I've always said that every day is a gift. The COVID pandemic pushed all of us to, or past, our breaking points. Maybe it's pushed you past those points multiple times. My heart bleeds for you. What I've seen is that we are all in the presence of the **Unknown.** We do not know all the science yet. We do not know why COVID got politicized in the first place. We do not know what the future holds. We do not know yet why it almost killed me and barely touched my family. This is just one thing that has shaped the fabric of who I am.

In 2012 when my son was born, I almost died, anaphylactic on the operating table while vomiting simultaneously. My dad gave me the words to get me through, "you have to surrender to win." I repeated his words in my head as I guppy-breathed, as if through a straw. Slowly, it eased, and I did get to hold my son. Less than two years later, his sister was born, the second precious love. Every day since I found out I was pregnant with my son, I've worked to create a better life for him. I'm not perfect and I've stumbled. When I did, I acknowledged it, got back up, and tried again. In 2014, the multiple food allergies reared their ugly heads. We learned to overcome and adapt, just like Mom had.

Why do I tell you any of this? Do I want your pity? Absolutely not. Do I want attention? No. My whole life I've hidden in the shadows, so I didn't have attention. I let fear win for far too long. It cost me greatly. That will not fly anymore. I am telling you all we've been through these last years and where my mother had been prior to her passing, so you know how triumphant not giving up can be. Until you know the journey one has taken, you cannot understand the path.

The truth is that we all have our stories, right? We all have unique journeys on this earth and unique timeframes. We don't know when it's over until it happens to us. We don't know what the miracle was until it's already happened usually. Sometimes, we also see the rainbows and ladybugs as miracles, signs from heaven, and know that we are loved beyond our understanding. Miracles do happen, large and small every day.

Over the years I've allowed my life to be run by anger, fear, love, and trust. I've chosen different things many times without being aware of the choice. Sometimes I felt that I had no choice at all. In the space of such terrible confinement and constraint, I felt hopeless even.

The tests we face are as innately individual and yet so very similar in theme and fundamental nature. We, as humans tend to feel, act, and behave as if we are the only ones on the planet who have ever been through anything ever. I am just as guilty of this as anyone else. I'm a survivor. One of my core mantras in life used to be that I could do anything, fight through anything by myself. It kept me very alone.

I've seen the lowest lows and felt empty inside. I could list all the reasons in the world and have in some cases already done just that. The truth is that my path has been mine to travel. Yes, I alone made my choices. That is not the same thing as being totally, completely, unequivocally alone in the world. I've met some people that deliberately chose alone knowingly. Deep in their eyes is that longing for something more, just like the most extroverted souls I've met. Connection with others does not have to equal weakness.

When you find someone who is contented with who they are and in the body they reside, it's like finding a diamond in the rough, an Australian opal in a vein of rocks. The peace and love that emanated from the Dalai Lama the day I heard him speak at Cornell was palpable. The thunder and lightning overhead did not dampen the moment. Rather, they electrified the energy and seemed to amplify his love and peace and joyful message. Being in his presence, even from a football field away, was miraculous. The peace was palpable. We basked in it gratefully.

For years, I lived in my cocoon. I created myself as small and unseen. The survivor inside told me that I had to, in order to survive. The survivor's guilt inside told me that I didn't deserve to be happy. That was all just a story that I made up. As my father passed away, I opened the doors to reality of what actually happened, rather than the stories I told myself. I opened the door over time and in ways that felt safe.

Mental health professionals are a great resource for many people. They exist for very important reasons. They help people work through their own doors systematically in safe ways. My father got so much

Overcoming

support and created so much positive movement in his own life with his therapist.

I however, did it on my own. I do not advocate one certain way. If you're ready to emerge as a butterfly, then I commend you. If you're still in your cocoon, I get that too. When you're ready, the Universe will open up for you in miraculous ways you cannot imagine. Parts of the process may be painful. Parts may be embarrassing, uncomfortable and yes, especially vulnerable. And this, my dear one, is where that elusive marrow of life lives. It does not live on the edge of one's sleeve. It's way down deep in the parts we do not often show the world. If you can have the courage to expose yourself that way, to speak your truth, have your voice heard, then you have life full of Soul Fire.

I am aware that I was very lucky as a young child. I've seen how devastating it can be for people when they do not feel loved or wanted. It can color your whole world view very differently. If you did not feel that same unconditional love when you were young, I am so sorry. You deserve love and light just as every other person on this earth.

We are meant to be beacons of love, the Dalai Lama says. Look for the answers you seek. They are inside of you, more often than not. Look for your role models. Find what helps you create your own peace. Do more of that.

Each person takes on very unique things from their experiences. When I took a nature photography class, the instructor reminded us that we can't help but be unique. Eight people stood at the lookout to the Smoky Mountains, side by side. Eight people made completely different choices about how to frame the shot, the settings, and all the details they included. Each of the photos were completely unique even though they were of the same gorgeous vista. What works for you may or may not work for me. That's okay.

It isn't about winning some elusive game. It's about what you gain, and sometimes what you lose, when you follow your path. People will notice the freedom you gain as a result of losing that old baggage. They will see who you actually are, rather than the person wading through the swamp of their old stuff. Your feet will feel more firmly planted wherever you are when you do. The change may be both profound and quiet as a whisper. I'm beginning to think some of the best changes are both.

Humanity is more resilient than we give ourselves credit for. Events, traumas, and life experiences change us. Sometimes, it feels like we've been completely torn to shreds. If our lives were a piece of fabric, then it had been cut up by a tiny toddler with adult scissors. Upon the realization that the precious cloth is no longer whole, we are torn. Sometimes we are utterly undone by what happens. It can take a while to stop our heads from spinning.

It took me a long time to process the events of my teen years. I stayed in denial for a very long time. If I did not admit that I was scared, then I could not be harmed. Yet, the emotions rotted and festered under the surface. It's only now that I'm realizing that I was never meant to put that fabric back together exactly as it was before the events. It took as long as it took for me to be willing to look. There is no blame or shame about that timing. I would not be who I am without my prior choices.

The fallacy in overcoming adversity is that there's a magic button that you can push, or a secret potion to mend the fabric into a perfect whole shape. We think that if we do it right, then the grief is no longer there. Denial held up this fallacy for me for several decades. It was only after a series of shredding events that I saw clearly. I sat on the metaphorical floor of my life and stared at this precious garment. It was as if I opened my eyes for the first time when my father died.

It was only when I was completely exhausted from circling my own drain that I did something to change it. I began to braid my shredded fabric into a long braid. It had new structure and strength, but no form. It felt like I was braiding forever.

At some point, when I looked all around me, there were no shredded parts any longer. I looked at the mile-long braid and asked what was next. Slowly, the parts got wound around in a circle, like a braided rug. The thread carefully chosen; I stitched them together piece by piece. At the end, there was a cohesive single unit again. Then I set to work with the fabric dye and the pattern.

Now, when I look back at the things that happened, I do not shake. I am not torn to shreds. I see that I have not completely erased all traces of any trauma that ever happened to me. Rather, I have woven a new fabric that is my life.

There comes a time in every person's life when they are tested. Life, circumstances, and sometimes people are put in our paths for a reason, I believe. These moments become pivot points from which we choose who we are. They define us unconsciously. Unless we really choose to look at each of them in turn, they can unwittingly run our very being.

The question to ask is where are you on your path? Are you ready to overcome? What tools do you already have at your disposal that you're underappreciating? What tools do you want to seek out help in order to grow? Our life skills are like the tools of any other trade. If you need a new tool, give yourself permission to go get it. You may seek multiple times until you find the tools that are a fit for the skill you're trying to hone. There is beauty in all of it. You're worth it.

It isn't about winning some elusive game. It's about what you gain, and sometimes what you lose, when you follow your path.

Choose To Live

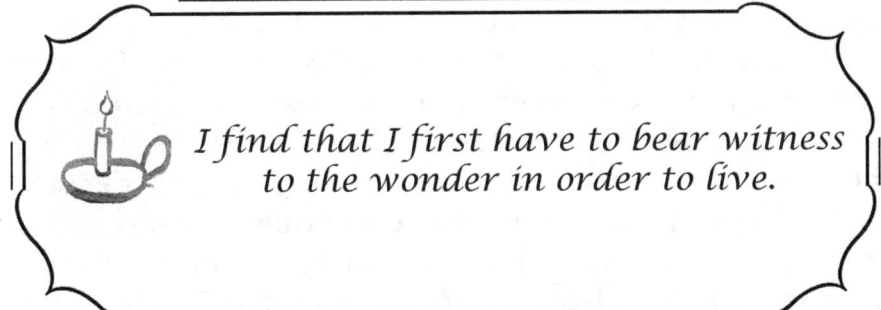

I find that I first have to bear witness to the wonder in order to live.

Soul Fire

My sincere and solemn hope is that we rise from the burning ashes with our eyes and our hearts open. Maybe you lost your business and half your family in the same month. Maybe you lost your husband or wife. Maybe you lost your sense of security and the eternal sunshine that you once had. In each and every place where the darkness has touched you, I acknowledge you for rising. I acknowledge you for doing the best you could to see your own light, find your own light.

There are times when life is terrible, horrifically terrible. There are times we bring it on ourselves and others where we simply do not have control over any of it. We get to choose who we are in each and every one of those moments. We get to say if we let the warmth of the sun reach our heart as it reaches our skin. We get to say if we are willing to let the past go. We get to say. You get to say. Now. You get to say in the next breath and the next and the next. Choose well. Make your choice worthy of your time.

The Unknown is a place that we are not innately comfortable with as humans. That's where the magic of life happens. As a child, my family took a trip over Christmas break to where Maine bordered Canada. We drove 800 miles to our destination. Upon arriving, the thermometer read minus twenty-eight degrees Fahrenheit. There was no cable television. Internet did not exist. Until that point, we had taken summer trips to the beach where I made sandcastles on the seashore. We traveled to the far north of the United States instead during the middle of winter.

Waking up surrounded by snow laden evergreen trees at eight years old, I was enchanted. The snow sparkled. The icicles were taller than I was at the time.

Suddenly, it hit me, I could build a snow castle. Shortly thereafter, I begged my dad to walk across the lake following the snowmobile path. We walked out to the middle of the lake holding hands like two little kids, rather than one. In stark contrast, my mom was huddled, shivering by the fire, utterly miserable. She didn't like these new circumstances.

In the moments, like with Dad on that frozen lake, true living happens. I find that I have to first bear witness to the wonder. When I realized as a child in Maine that I got to decide my own attitude, I was free to be happy. Yes, I was cold. It was the coldest temperatures I've ever experienced. Yet, the sun shone and there was more snow than any child could ever need to build a castle. There was joy. There was love. We explored. I chose to be happy when I sat there shivering at the fireplace, warming my fingers and toes. I chose. This trip is one of my favorite memories. For the first time in my life, I realized I could choose how to frame my experience of the world.

I have also fallen down, hidden under the covers and yelled "No! No! No!", like a child. Now I realize that I chose **those** moments too.

Our bathroom fell apart during 2020. We could have superglued the fallen tile back to the wall, painted the tiles white, or ignored it altogether. We chose to renovate. In the months that followed, we carved out the life we wanted deliberately, rather than just accepting the one we were dealt.

Rule one of renovations is that rebuilding is messy. That's true in life as well. My friend Lisa said, "The journey to change is never pretty." When renovating one's life, the journey is not a pristine yellow brick road. It's a winding road through the woods, past grandmother's house, and definitely the road less traveled. Sometimes the brush gets so thick you can barely see the forest through the trees. Too much? Not really. Digging deep into your soul requires faith and a lot of metaphors.

You must have faith that the outcome you visualize is possible. Each step turns out differently than we typically imagine it as well. Yet, what we learn through the process of living our lives cannot be handed over without walking the path. The knowledge is acquired with time, and cultivation, much like the tomatoes in the garden.

One year after my mother's passing, the whole room had been pulled down to the studs and the subfloor. Roofing paper was underneath the vanity, along with an old newspaper remnant dated 1981. I guess the vanity hadn't been original. That tile sure was original and built bomb shelter style. Looking around the room, I thought that it had good bones. I began envisioning what it could look like. I began to dream.

How long does the dreaming phase last exactly? I'm asking for a friend. Ours lasted nine months and went through a handyman, a plumber/contractor, and then a contractor-plumber-tiler dream team. Third time's a charm they say. For our bathroom, this was also the case. Once again, when your gut instinct says *call person X,* usually that person is the right one for the job. COVID delayed many things. The first two people we called were slammed busy for months. The day I accepted the bid for the contractor's plumber, the first plumber came to look at the house again. Life can be funny like that.

Our dreaming phase was like growing and birthing a child. At first, we compared the child to fruit and it was an abstract thought. Then, as the wall came down, and the foundation was built, the child was growing. My inner child was being healed with this project. There was no coffin shower anymore. The contractor reframed the shower so the ceiling went the full height, eight feet like the rest of the bathroom. The olive green was gone. Piece by piece we picked each item, from the white tile, marble, and vanity to the shower head. Each item felt as though one more piece was being set right. Choosing the vanity took two months. At first, we had settled for the cherry finish of the mahogany because the piece looked very much like our bedroom furniture. By the time we were ready to begin, they sold the exact one we wanted in the white we wanted. The small size of the room made a white vanity so much more appealing. We didn't have to settle for something we didn't really want. We really could have the bathroom we preferred.

When the contractor came, things moved so fast, my body could barely keep up. It was beautiful to watch the love and care that the plumber and especially the tile guys put into the bathroom. Each piece was carefully selected to enhance the pattern and design. The white shower tile resembled marble and had gray veining throughout. Each cut was carefully considered, then cut once and installed. It was a work of art. At the end of the week, the tile gleamed back at me from all angles. The wall color we'd selected went well with the shampoo niche glass tiles, the blues and greens of the ocean. The color selection was as precise as every other choice had been. Hundreds of light blue green options later, we chose one called "Swimming." It most resembled the color of the water in Destin, Fl. Color, like food, evokes memories for me. That specific blue green shade, and only that one fit the bill perfectly.

Houses all need love along the way. Moving into one is like getting another full-time job you never get paid for. Cultivating it the way you actually want it is key.

When we moved into the house, we removed the huge flowered wallpaper from the stairway and the upstairs hallway. The next step after that, we never did. Life happened. We were raising two children and my husband was finishing his Navy career. On that week, we completed a project that was seven years in the making. We primed and painted the stairway and hallway walls.

Primer is a stinky process at best. The oil-based primer is a necessary evil to fully prepare plaster walls to accept paint after wallpaper. The glue from wallpaper, oil-based paint, and wood stain all change the colors of wall paints unless you prime it properly.

The weather broke from winter for a three-day stint just as the tile guys finished. It was fortuitous. That blue painter's tape was lovingly laid on those stairs months before. Completing this step felt like finishing a chapter in our lives. It took a lot longer than planned. It was messy. The results were worth it. Renovating our bathroom was like the healing process. At a time when very little of life was normal, and change was thrust upon us, we altered our own space. We picked one thing we could affect and chose deliberately.

The way I saw it is that we can pretend things are the same. We can pretend that politics haven't gotten painfully oppositional. Or we could choose to sit down at the table with people we may not agree with and listen. We can stand up for humanity and say the difficult things respectfully. We can stand up for ourselves, equality, and our fellow humans. We can choose to let love in and push away hatred. We can choose to be the light. We can all choose to live life now, and every single day. Choosing to live can be about things outside ourselves.

Human nature wants to help people, and yet when threatened and pushed to the edge, our questions show. Our questions about life and humanity, science, politics, and religion are natural queries about our place in the world. We land wherever we land on those issues. We do not have to let it keep us separate from those we love. The pandemic realities have been hard enough, in my mind, and we get to choose if we are going to learn from the past and be honest with ourselves or not.

I chose to live life. For a year, that meant taking my time climbing up the stairs. I choose love. Love is everywhere if we look. Please don't misunderstand me. Choosing to see the light does not under any circumstances mean that I choose to ignore the presence of the darkness or even the grief. It meant that I allowed those moments as they came and yet did not dwell in them. It meant that I tried to emulate Rudyard Kipling's "If" poem rather than point the fingers everywhere else but inward. It's a lot easier said than done.

It means that even as I push myself to the limits of what my body says I can handle today, I'm aware they'll be different tomorrow. Having symptoms post COVID means I've gotten used to the dreaded unknown. I choose that deliberately though. I decide to take part in life, rather than to wait for death. I choose to live rather than merely survive. I choose every day to climb the stairs of my health. I have no idea where the top of the landing is located. Some days, I don't even know where the top of the next step is, or how long the tread will be. I may have to climb for weeks to get a new health level, to stop wheezing when I do this or that for example. I may have to rest for days afterwards.

I listen to my body. It's quite loud these days anyway. It's easy to hear. Resting is sometimes an absolute requirement. When I've rested enough, I know. And I rise.

Sometimes, we look at life, whatever's around us and everything just seems tough. Even things that used to be simple seem insurmountable. At times like these, we wish life was easy. On one hand, it occurs like the best things in life have been worked for. On the other hand, when I've been ready to tackle a thing, it has actually been easy to see the next step. Maybe the secret to something feeling easy is simply being ready.

It may take time to accomplish that thing you want in life. The bachelor's degree and master's degrees don't just happen. We make them a priority in life and do the work to make them a reality. The journey of anything worth doing is not typically instantaneous. Along the way, we get opportunities to learn, grow, and evolve.

Lately, the focus for me has been on all the places I unintentionally chose. I decided to let go of the past rather than hold on to it for dear life. I realized that the holding on kept me dead inside anyway. I acknowledge my past self for what I've been through, to see it for what it was, and to let it go.

It's as if I wanted to go on a camping trip. There were things to manage, things to do in order to go camping and be prepared. First, I picked where I was going, my clothes, gear, and food. I planned routes to get there perhaps. Each part had something to manage about it. When I really wanted to go camping, this process seemed easy usually.

Choose To Live

If I dreaded camping though, I may drag my feet and do all kinds of things to avoid said trip. To what end? If I chose to go, then I go. Or not. This personal metamorphosis was like that for me as well.

Along the way, I've seen bits and pieces and sometimes huge mountains where I've held myself back. Many times, it felt like I'd been walking while looking at the ground and just looked up for the first time to see a mountain in front of me. Sometimes it was a cliff's edge. Barely catching my steps before I stepped off the cliff unaware, I often gasped in surprise. Remembering that I chose this journey, I looked and decided where I wanted to go next. It was all unknown, unfamiliar territory. That's where the magic happened.

Walking with my mother in her final months was miraculous. Over the years, I found and cultivated forgiveness with her. We had a real, fulfilling, loving relationship as a result. We got to spend time together, catching up and making up for lost time. We held it for what it was, a gift of time. When my mother did something, she usually did it big. Her last year was no different.

All along the way, there were miracles, signs, and angels. That journey could've been spent very differently by each of us quite easily. We chose miraculous. We chose that we would spend each day as fully as we could doing what we wanted to do together. As fate would have it, the pandemic shut down many of my other outside responsibilities right at that same time. We had time together. Every rainbow, ladybug, and sign from Above filled us with that same Universal love and Dalai Lama level joy.

We were aware and accepted that there was no conservation of joy or of love. That meant there was no real cap on how much love or joy we were able to feel. I've seen children who operated from this thought pattern and believed that there is a 'good one' and a 'bad one.' They believed that if their sibling was doing so well in so many areas, then they had to fill the role of the 'bad one.' That flawed logic, as my husband so wisely pointed out, is not reality. It's just something that our children made up while comparing themselves harshly to each other.

There is only the constraint we place on our own thoughts, feelings, and actions. That's not to say that the laws of physics don't exist. They are real. Science is real. I see the power of our thoughts in action too in my life. I see how my way of being in the world affect, color, and shade every step I take. I see how I choose to live.

Falling can be our biggest asset sometimes. In my world, it usually seems like a curse at the time, but it's within the moments where I see who I am, that I get to choose differently. It's within the vulnerable places, and often the frustration, that I can see the path through the forest.

No matter what you believe, no matter what you experience, at the end of the day you decide what living looks like. You get to choose.

Choosing to see the light does not under any circumstances mean that I choose to ignore the presence of darkness or even the grief. It meant that I allowed those moments as they came and yet did not dwell in them.

Aneurysm Alley

The pattern of my life would repeat until I dealt with it. I could hide the trauma behind that huge steel door. The fear remained stuck to me like a lead weight. It colored all my other choices for as long as I let it remain.

Soul Fire

The military service did not threaten my husband John's life. The aneurysm and strokes threatened to take him. For several years, every moment of every day, I lived with a disturbingly high amount of cortisol, a.k.a. stress hormone.

In 2015, my dad, who'd lived with us had emergency aneurysm surgery on his abdominal aortic aneurysm (AAA). Two days later came my husband's stroke. That's right, He had a full-blown stroke at thirty something. 2015 to 2017 were spent praying, holding our breath, and searching for answers.

I opened my eyes and exhaled. I could do this. I had to be strong for the children. They were so young. They were three and almost two years old. How could they ever understand what just happened?

I was a stay-at-home mother who kept the house going and took care of my father and two children. My bachelor's degrees wouldn't sustain us if John couldn't work. Sometimes, the weight of the world was so heavy that I could only work in small increments. That's all I really got anyway, the present. One more deep breath in and out as I passed the nurses desk, and the three of us walked into his hospital room.

I set our youngest, our daughter, down on his bed with him. She fell into his arms like butter melting into freshly made toast. She only saw him. My son's eyes widened at all things in the room, how different Daddy looked, and his very odd gown. Lord, I remember the moment I found out my own father had his first stroke. I was an adult in college. Our children were babies. Sometimes life can seem so cruel.

Most of us can recall the moment the rock in our family went from being superhuman to human and vulnerable. For me with my husband, it was the strokes. He was the make it happen man. He could make anything happen, juggle a million projects at once, and remember it all. He was the one who the Navy deemed worthy to study his Master's degree, on the Navy's dime, in both Monterey, CA and Singapore. He got to be an ambassador for the brightest and someone who improved international relations with Singapore. Not many got this opportunity for dual master's degrees from Naval Postgraduate School. They're very selective in the first place with whom they allow into their programs. Now my personal super-man had to ring a call bell to get up to pee. What was this world coming to? Whose life did I wake up in? It didn't feel like mine.

Our lives hung on a spider's filament. The fate of his career hung in the balance of his recovery and what came next. His Commanding Officer and Executive Officer would decide whether he would be allowed to stay in the Navy at all, let alone on that ship. They fought to keep him.

The sun glints on a spider's web and makes it look fragile. Spider silk is incredibly durable and resilient, however. It has great strength that is not visible to the human eye. The webs are especially beautiful in the backdrops of the mountains and the morning fog. Dew drops hang beneath the intricately woven geometric patterns of the spider's web. Sometimes we are the spider, weaving. Sometimes we are the dew drops. Yet other times, we are the webs strung from point to point, woven around structures and circumstances already in place. I had grown used to trusting someone, believe it or not. As much as it stretched my soul to trust and be vulnerable; it had become comfortable.

The cardiologist said what most had said, "There's nothing more I can do for you."

Being the fighter I am, I sat up straighter, looked him in the eye, and asked him what any good pre-med wife would ask, "Who's next? Who is the next person on the list that can find these answers for him?" That question confronted their egos and their medical knowledge. Most importantly though, it made them ask the questions themselves.

If they weren't going to figure it out then darn it, I would. I went to work and used everything I'd ever learned about people and medicine in my years of college. I fought hard for my husband's life and for the next referral. I fought so our children would have a father. I fought so hard that I forgot how to be a wife.

Not one of the doctors had seen a case like his before. Some at the hospital had seen strokes in young men. However, it was exceedingly rare. None of them had a cure or a fix. The best they ever came up with was telling him "Don't put up too many blinds or look up a lot. It could cause a stroke." The recurrent word every doctor said was idiopathic. In other words, the medical community did not know why he kept having strokes before the age of forty.

Each doctor looked at me and my husband and said, "I don't know what's causing these strokes." I immediately replied, "Ok, who's the next doctor that does know the answer?" An MRI finally showed a tiny pencil line in one artery that fed the brain. It was below the area of the strokes. They thought it was an aneurysm but couldn't be sure. Several specialists later, including the Hematology/Oncology doctor, we found our answer and our doctor. The vascular surgeon at the Naval hospital knew the vascular brain surgeon for the job, an interventional radiologist vascular surgeon.

After his sixth stroke, we finally got a referral to the civilian doctor who would be his brain surgeon. The doctor walked in with a bowl of candy and asked if we wanted some. He didn't flaunt his Harvard or Yale degrees, though he had them. Bless that man, three and a half hours later, he answered every question I had that no one could answer in the two years prior. He was kind, caring, and above all honest.

He was the self-proclaimed "brain plumber" for the job of fixing my husband's remarkably gifted brain. The best news was that he could fix it. There was a tiny "pipeline" stent that he placed inside his blood vessel. No big deal. That vessel fed his brainstem where his brain told him to breathe and his heart to beat. The doctor made it seem simple. Yet, he had all the ethics and humbleness and authenticity about the reality of the situation. It was unknown.

Once again, I had to live inside the unknown. *Why me,* I asked. Apparently, I had things to learn inside the unknown.

It took two years, a dozen doctors, and several dozen tests. To John's recollection, in the month following the last stroke, they took forty-eight vials of blood to find the answers. Those are just the vials he was conscious for. The surgery to correct his pseudoaneurysm took place early 2017 and was successful. My husband had a stent placed by the doctor that healed that artery and allowed him to live.

Six months later, my father died because his AAA replacement surgery was ultimately not able to save him. They did their absolute best, but Dad lost six liters of blood on the table. He only had ten liters in his whole body. He couldn't regain strength to get off the ventilator. Two days before he died, Dad said to me in a whisper, "I'm checkin' out." Three failed extubations later, he did "check out" at 11:11 PM. His birthday was November eleventh.

We may not have control over the entirety, but I believe we can steer the outcomes of our lives in the directions we choose. Dad showed me that.

I refused to deal with something and only delayed that inevitable reality when that door was in my face, yet again. Sometimes, for an added bonus feature, I got more of the same in different circumstances. As a teen, I refused to be a victim. I refused to make it easy to be killed. I was a survivor.

What I would not do was admit that I had been scared. Admitting that truth in my faulty logic meant that I had been a victim. The lie that I told myself was that if I didn't admit it, then it didn't happen.

The truth was that it was terrifying. There was a period of time as a teenager when I didn't know If I'd wake up in the morning. It lasted for almost a year. That was the first time. Even when the restraining order came through, it wasn't over for me. I built the door then. I created it with all the emotions I had.

The cycle continued with my husband years later. From day to day, I didn't know if he would survive. That pattern would repeat until I dealt with it. I could hide the trauma behind that huge steel door. The fear remained stuck to me like a lead weight. It colored all my other choices for as long as I let it remain.

There were two solid years of my life where I did not know if my husband would wake up in the morning. I had chosen to follow him through his military career around the country. I chose that over going to medical school and finishing my education. Choosing to fully trust and rely on another soul was one of the hardest things I've ever done in my life. I didn't always succeed either.

When a giant falls, the ground doubtlessly ripples as they crash hard to the ground. There were so many things to be grateful for following John's stroke. The slurring stopped. He could speak clearly. He could walk and talk well in spite of the strokes being in that part of the brain. He could still write computer programming, a.k.a. code.

In the early days, the vertigo was really intense for him. Everything caused overstimulation. The movement of the cars on the highway as we rounded an entrance ramp almost made him puke the first time. The ripples in our world were subtle and also devastating.

The children playing became noise that rendered him useless. The sounds bombarded his brain as he tried to walk or talk and were instantly too much. The saddest and hardest parts of those moments for me were how it affected my children and that he did not recognize it at all.

Grief was not something my husband was accustomed to, or educated in. There was grief with the strokes. It was too intense for him to admit for a while. I tried to give him space. He built red oak shelves in the library during his mandatory thirty days off for recovery with the Navy. As that first month waned, we had to have our first come to Jesus talk about his recovery and what it would look like.

As his wife, I had to step in and ask him to look at his grief. I had to ask him to look under the rocks he'd immediately hidden away. For the first time, he acted like a typical man. Providing for his family was very important, vital even, to him. Being faced with that being threatened, he was undone.

Standing in our kitchen over the multi colored brown and tan granite island, I squared my shoulders and stood up straight. The sun came in from the window behind me, illuminating his surly frame and arms crossed over his chest. He was not happy. He did not want to look in this place. Secretly, I didn't blame him one bit. I didn't want to have this conversation. I wanted to be anywhere else doing anything else. Yet, there I was. I asked him to put his heart into physical therapy even if it seemed stupid to walk a straight line. I reiterated what the doctors and nurses had said and what I knew as a scientist about recovery. If he ever wanted to walk a straight line again, or to stop having the vertigo, then he had to push himself.

Even as he dug his heels more firmly into the shiny hardwood floors, he promised that he would try. He didn't want to. He wanted to scream about the unfairness of it all. And he knew that the only way out of this place was through. Both our fathers had massive strokes by this time. He was probably comparing himself to both of them. One lost all speech entirely and suffered from apraxia and aphasia. The other struggled hard to walk on his own two feet. To the untrained eye, and sometimes the trained eye, my husband looked entirely normal. Normal was a word I have never understood or resonated with. In this moment, that was no different.

Over the course of the next two years, my husband worked hard to push himself on the boundaries of his stroke. At first, he tested the waters angrily and with trepidation. As the vertigo thankfully lessened, he was also better able to walk straight. He passed the necessary Naval requirements and finished his tour on the ship he was assigned to. The new navigator got to take the ship into the Mediterranean though. For John, this was a slap in the face, a final blow of sorts.

Outwardly, he showed his bravery and courage and will to survive. Inwardly, he was crushed. He had been in the Navy for eighteen years and seen nearly every ocean it had to offer. He'd seen every ocean, except the Mediterranean. "Each one has a different color," he'd say with a gleam and love in his eyes, "They're unique and each beautiful in their own right." He spoke about the oceans as he spoke about a secret lover. And he did so without looking me in the eyes. He couldn't look at me in those moments of deep sharing. For him, he felt like he was betraying me and his whole family to love the ocean and being at sea so much.

It was frankly miraculous that the Navy didn't kick him off the ship entirely when they'd found four strokes. Two years later, stroke six happened with a silent fifth in between. During those two years, he saw neurologists, cardiologists, a hematologist/oncologist, and finally a vascular surgeon.

In the middle of Aneurysm Alley, Jen, my soul sister was right beside me. One day, while I was venting about everything, she stopped me midsentence, "Some things are so big that if you blink too long, then you'll be taken under. Let's go paint pottery." I saw the visual of the life raft for the first time. She'd been through big things in life. She'd seen me cry, scream, and have my pity parties. She and my cousin stood beside us questioning, praying, and crying. Jen didn't want to paint that day because it was her deepest desire in life.

She painted with me so we didn't drown in the enormity of it all.

My husband would never have chosen a single stroke for himself. He didn't want the uncertainty or the exploration of self, to be honest. He didn't want to learn how to grieve. He didn't want to be a one in a billion statistic. It was in those very things that he discovered himself though. He discovered his own inner strength and forged it through his own fire.

That fall, if you will, all the medical issues, gave rise to a new passion in woodworking. He began to create something spectacular to house his beloved books. He may have been fueled by anger at the time. The red oak wall to wall bookshelves were stunning. They were also his outlet during those first thirty days post stroke.

It would take two years to leave the emergency crisis management mode of Aneurysm Alley. The day I stopped my own inner whirlpool of chaos was the day I knew he would live. That was six months after his last stroke. Some days, we both have to remember that we are not back there, in that timeframe. When you're so used to one way of life, it can be tough to change. Some days, I force myself to realize that there isn't a fight for someone's life currently happening.

Choosing to live isn't about doing the easy thing. It's definitely not about doing what we've always done. Choosing to live is digging down really deep and doing the healthy thing for yourself, even if it's hard. It requires change. As my friend Lindsey so keenly stated, "we can't save ourselves unless we make that choice. To so many people (including myself, sometimes) change is the enemy." Lindsey is a brilliant person who knows herself better than most. Hard-earned insight can be a superpower.

Aneurysm Alley

There are some people who lose the battle regardless of how hard their loved ones tried. An assumption by those who honestly don't know any better is that no one tried to get them help. People who have not been touched by suicide may think that someone didn't try hard enough. That's simply not usually true. I personally know people who did everything they could for years to get their loved ones help. It did not work. It is important to offer grace to those who've taken their own lives, as well as to their loved ones, rather than judgment. People's lives are like fingerprints.

If you had told me when I sat there with a knife to my wrist at sixteen to choose life, I probably would've gone through with it just to spite you. The anger at Nightmare Man winning if I died is what personally fueled me at that time. Now that I am more healed, I can see more, look deeper, and hopefully open doors that were previously closed.

When something doesn't touch your life and completely alter it, we don't know what to say. Sometimes people say things that really hurt people who have lost loved ones. It's usually completely unintentional.

When someone is scared all the time, they don't think they have a choice. They don't see a way out. It's important that I bring awareness to this with sensitivity for all those who lost their battles.

It pisses me off to read the disclaimers to just seek therapy like it's a one size fix all. Therapy can be a helpful tool for most. It is not always the only path.

I know that save yourself isn't the therapy sound way. I also know that on some level, we all are tasked with saving ourselves from the fear and darkness. This doesn't mean that you need to or even should do it all on your own. The healthy thing we may need to do could be therapy. Why should we deny ourselves help, if we need it? Why should addressing the needs of the brain be any different than treating the ailments of the body? Are they not equally as important in living a healthy, whole life?

Change is the enemy because it brings up all the fear, doubt, and for some of us, fight or flight reflexes. It's comfortable where we know the outcomes. It's much easier to suffer than it is to alter our own course. I spent more than half my life in an unalterable state. It did not serve me.

I did not die because I said yes to people. I did not die because my fear told me I would. Most of the bad things that my hard-working brain told me could happen in what if scenarios have not come to pass. It also took the tsunami of my parents dying and my husband's strokes in order to move me from where I stood. I totally understand that change is not easy. It is worth it. My path of overcoming had a lot of bends in the road. It required more persistence than I knew I had. Overcoming also required a magnifier to view into my own part in the whole. Sometimes the light through the magnifier burnt a bit. It was also vital to getting unstuck.

Aneurysm Alley tested my husband, myself, and the whole family to the brink. I had to surrender to live through losing my father. I had to realize that stress could kill me. I had to walk through the doors of my past traumas because they burst wide open. My husband's health called into question every decision I'd made to trust someone with everything. I had to deal with my own hiding mechanisms, anxieties, and fears. I had to look at forgiveness to weave our lives back together. That all had to start with me first before I could give the lessons to my young children. I had to celebrate every step, deal with my grief, and remember to play, dance, and to live. This collective is my definition of overcoming.

The big things require many tools. There were times that I had to be okay with not being okay. When others who loved me deeply reassured me in the face of the unknown and unfixable, I allowed myself to not be reassured. I prepared for all possibilities because it was the honest thing to do. When the relentless crashing of waves ceased, I began proverbial clean up and healing.

My husband had to do his own version of all these steps. He healed, mended, and processed his own way. He retreated inward, built red oak bookshelves, and eventually walked the floorboards of our back porch. He used his anger as fuel for the fire while he did the physical therapy. He worked hard to heal physically. He looked in the closets he didn't want to deal with and found his own way back to health. He found new grace for himself he never knew he needed.

It pried open the old steel door, ripped out my heart, and broke me a thousand times over, as a friend said. I rebuilt that boat. I rebuilt my life. John rebuilt his piece by piece as well. Thankfully, we had help. Thankfully, we were willing to see that help and accept it when offered. We may have fussed at the same time. We still did so just in time.

Some things require everything we have. Just when you think you can't give one more ounce, you dig deeper. Make that life raft. Build the good into your life with all the healthy tools at your disposal. Accept yourself. Allow for your feelings. All of them. Build as long and as fast as you can. Process, rest, and repeat if you must. You know what your body needs. You can tell the difference between unhealthy coping mechanisms and giving each emotion its turn on the stage. Aneurysm Alley taught me about my capacities.

Jen didn't want to paint pottery that day because it was her deepest desire in life. She painted with me so we didn't drown in the enormity of it all.

Just in Time

Whenever I have ignored the urge that the Universe placed in my path, things didn't go well.

Do you ever feel like things work out just in time? Or that you got what you needed at the exact right moment? Some people call it serendipity. Others call it God winks. I just call it my life. Magic happens over and over again when your heart is open and you are authentic with other humans.

When I had no more fight to give, a soul sister like Jen or Lisa came along. They helped carry the burdens that I was empty from carrying. They held me when I cried. They listened, which helped me make sense of the insane situations I found myself facing. They came just in time, every time.

No matter what has ever happened, deep down, I had an inner knowing. Underneath the action, under the drama, there was a still small voice that told me it would be okay. That obstacle was put in place for a reason. I could choose to learn and grow from it. Or, sometimes, if I had a particularly harsh case of the "I don't wannas", I could ignore it. Whenever I have ignored the urge that the Universe placed in my path, things didn't go well. That very same situation showed up in my life repeatedly until I said yes. Whether you believe this is the work of God, the Universe, or nothing at all is perfectly alright. I personally believe that there are things I'm meant to learn in this life.

Every single piece of the puzzle that was my father's passing seemed to be engineered for everyone involved to learn things. My father had to let go of control. I, by extension had to let go of control as well. Watching his body fail, I had the opportunity to see that his death was not my personal failure. My cousin reminded me kindly that I was not God. I did not have that power. I laughed with tears in my eyes when he said those very real and kind words. Even Dad's surgeons did not have the ultimate say. The web of life is so delicately woven, it's hard to see sometimes. When the light hits it all just right, and the sunlight comes over the hill behind it, the whole web gets illuminated.

I cannot count the amount of walks I took with my friend Lisa, pondering life. I can tell you firmly and without reservation that each one of them saved me. Every day, walking with my mom through her cancer and last months took every ounce of energy I had. The walks helped me to fill my bucket again. The life force mana was poured over me from the top of my head to the tip of my toes. It didn't matter how many steps we took or even how long they lasted. Each one was perfectly created to breathe life into us both. We had no clue in 2020 how long it would last. My mother had no idea how long her time on this earth was. Deep down, she knew it was short. She lived in each moment every day.

When we each lay our heads on our pillows at night, do we ask ourselves what we've done with that day's gift? I think we all have a deeper understanding of mortality and the fragility of life. Do we have a deep knowing of how beautiful it all is though?

I said *No* to the Universe a lot over the years. In my desperate, fervent drive to hide, I said no to my life. There were Universities that were fabulous for dance and for art. I wanted to go to several of them. I secretly really wanted my sculpture to be seen at the MOMA. I said no to all of that. It made me miserable to say no to my dreams when I knew better. It didn't do me any good. However, without each and every decision I've ever made, I would not be where I am right now today. I'm grateful.

Growth requires some measure of humility. What I am noticing when I'm in conversations that challenge me is that growth in any real sense of the word requires me to admit that I'm wrong about something. Either I have allowed an old memory to cloud the sight of my present or I simply made a mistake. Either way, swallowing one's pride is easier for some of us than others.

Asking hard questions about my life and desiring growth is like willingly walking over the hot coals of my past. At least for me, I am taken back to the moments that formed the stories or the places where I allowed the fear to win. It's like a time machine that transports my mind, body, and soul back to a very specific place and time. The real trick is not falling all the way into the rabbit hole.

Timing changes everything. Through some miracle, or a million, my husband survived and recovered well. He got to retire from the Navy after serving twenty years. If he had been in a different stage of his career, or not recovered exactly as much as he did, then he would not have been able to continue in the military. If I hadn't been a pre-medicine student, I doubt I would've known what questions to ask the doctors. If I wasn't ready to let go of the past wounds, then I'd be a much more traumatized adult trying hard to parent two beautiful children. If I hadn't healed some from the old wounds, who knows if I would've given up when I was so sick.

Every single time I opened the door to a specific topic, regardless of how long ago, the Universe provided that very thing in a new way. That very thing shows up in my life. If I write about listening for example, then listening situations show up all over in different places.

Just in Time

The converse is also true. Because my heart and soul are open to being molded into growing into what I was meant to become, I can hear it and I can see it. I was ready.

One day, Mr. Godsend said "imagine all of the things in your life that you would've missed if you were not fully present. Imagine how different your life would be." Imagine that indeed.

Growth in any real sense of the word requires me to admit that I'm wrong about something. Either I have allowed an old memory to cloud the sight of my present or I simply made a mistake. Either way, swallowing one's pride is easier for some of us than others.

Soul Fire

Signs and Miracles

Sometimes, when we most need them, the signs find us.

Soul Fire

As we travel our own roads, there are times we run out of gas. We find ourselves with an empty bucket and have no clue how to go on to the next step. In my life, when I've reached the end of my rope, there's always a kind hand, a sign or symbol, or even a miracle to help me back up. What helps you out of those moments is entirely unique to you. It's up to us to remember to open our eyes and our hearts to look for those gifts.

When my father died, I hadn't seen any monarch butterflies at all that year. One sunny day I was willing myself to inner peace with the sunshine on the back porch. As I sat on the screened in porch this unusually warm November day, I wondered if I should take the family to the cemetery to honor Dad for his birthday. As if my mind answered for him, I thought, *No, just enjoy good chocolate and be kind to each other.* That would make him happy. At precisely that moment by my left ear, carried on the warm moist wind, was a bright orange monarch butterfly. He answered my prayers with the flutter of his stunning wings. I'm grateful for the gift of these signs. I glanced left and smiled as I looked around. I gasped as two more monarchs fluttered by and circled one another in my backyard! That year I'd seen no monarchs. One sunny day when I least expected it, I saw three at once. My father was a numerologist and astrologer amongst other things. Three was his very favorite number in the entire world. For Dad, I knew the answer had to be chocolate because he loved it so very much. There were years he abstained from chocolate like he did from alcohol. He viewed it as a similar addiction. That's an addiction I can understand. I smiled and went inside to hug my family and make chocolate.

Signs and Miracles

My friend Emma called me to tell me that at that same exact time across the country, she had seen three ladybugs in a place she'd never seen them before. Dad loved that Emma called them ladybirds as she was from Australia. I had to share the story with my dad's younger sister. "What day? I saw a hummingbird at that same time, down at the beach house," she said. A hummingbird was on the front cover of my dad's poetry book. The time spent at the beach house was very special to them.

Three people close to Dad saw three different signs that were special to each of them at the same time on the same day in three different states. That type of sign was so strong, undeniable, and special to me. It gave me the gift of peace and a big smile I hadn't had in a long time, exactly when I needed it.

When life is dark, and seemingly hopeless or lifeless, or even relentless, be patient. It's hard as hell sometimes. There is life in the dark. We sometimes have to look harder for the light and the life we want.

Sometimes, when we most need them, the signs find us. March of 2020 brought the world to its knees. Lisa and I began taking walks together outside in our neighborhood. One such day in March, it was warm and sunny. We were walking and talking and destressing, just two moms. Often, we waxed philosophical. Lisa had always been a sounding board for whatever showed up in my heart and sometimes troubled soul.

The phone rang mid-walk. I knew. This was **THE** call. "Hi," Mom said slowly and deliberately with a sigh. "They called me with the brain MRI results today. There are three tumors in my brain. One is on the trigeminal nerve. One is in the cerebellum and one is in the frontal lobe. They want to start radiation immediately on the brain." That sunny St Patrick's Day suddenly didn't look so sunny. I stopped in my tracks.

I fell to my knees as my chest tightened with the gut-wrenching ache of grief. I told my mom outwardly that we'd get through it together. Inwardly, I was totally undone. The phone call was brief but heavier than lead. We stopped walking and found a grassy spot to sit near the nearby church.

I played Dad's songs for my friend, cried, reasoned, rationed out my feelings, and screamed. Just at that moment of breathlessness, I looked down right in front of me in the itchy green grass. There was a beautiful ladybug, crawling between my friend and I. For several very long minutes I played my dad's music and photographed that tiny ladybug with Lisa. When the sky began to look ominous and I'd emptied out for the moment, we went home.

A half an hour later, the sky was blue and thick with the storm clouds. The sky opened up and let out the thick wet warm tears from heaven. Thunder and lightning came. Right along with it came the bright sunshine. I looked outside where we had been with the ladybug and sure enough, there was a bright rainbow. "Lisa, check it out!" I texted.

"I see one too", she replied! "I'm photographing it right now in my street."

Immediately I picked up the phone and called Mom to tell her the story. "I see one here too," she said. Each of us was a mile or two apart. The conditions for all of us to see rainbows in three locations at the same time seemed impossible. I knew right then that whatever would happen along the way for Mom, it would be ok. We weren't alone.

Signs and Miracles

Every step of the way, including the day before Mom died, there were rainbows. Mom's breathing was terrible that day. She was weak in body, but strong in mind. Feeling hopeless as I left the hospital wondering if I'd see her alive again, I looked up. The rainbow was right there straight ahead of me as I left the hospital main entrance. It stretched in front of me across the whole sky. That rainbow gave me strength to call my sister to give her the update for the day. I walked over to my car and sat there numb as I recounted how Mom was doing. I looked up, blinded by my thick hot tears, in the parking lot. "Oh my Lord, there's the brightest rainbow I've ever seen!" There it was, indeed, a second rainbow sitting perpendicular to the first one I'd seen moments ago. This one was brighter and bigger than the first.

There are those who strongly believe that rainbows are God's promises. My mother is among them and she raised us that way. Every step of my mother's journey to the other side, there were signs, symbols, and little "God signs," as Lisa says. I chose to believe in the hope of that promise. In the end, Mom's passing was merciful, peaceful, and filled with her favorite quiet music of Roberta Flack.

The first holidays without Mom were hard. It was difficult to quantify which was the hardest. It's incredibly personal and dependent on the individual. Grief is love changed by death. It changes over time and still comes in waves regardless of how much time has passed. Easter was a larger wave of grief for our family in the wake of Mom's passing.

Easter was Mom's favorite holiday for as long as I could remember. She loved the resurrection story of Jesus and all the promise, hope, and love it brought every year. So naturally, the first Easter without her here brought some grief. Saturday before I was sad, missing her, and remembering taking her photos by the azaleas the previous Easter.

I forced myself to create the Easter meal, with my husband of course. The Easter bunny came as usual too. I remembered how every year, no matter how old I got, the Easter bunny came. We weren't poor when Easter came. We were simply protected and loved and joyous.

The weather echoed my mood. It was cold and cloudy outside. In my experience releasing butterflies, they usually emerged from cocoons on sunny days. The swallowtails that wintered over in the butterfly tent on our porch had no reason to emerge without the sun to warm them. The sun would give them energy to break free of the cocoon. And yet, there she was on Easter.

That beautiful black swallowtail butterfly was in her cocoon all winter, since mid-October the previous year. I snatched my full frame camera like any photographer would. I gave my daughter the phone so she could record a video. The butterfly's bodily fluids were still in her black abdomen. They had not fully filled out her wings yet. They couldn't yet be dry. However, she came out more than ready to fly! And fly she did!

She flew so fast that my daughter couldn't get her on video! She was free! She had waited, transformed, and emerged. She clearly thought she had waited long enough! The butterfly emerging on Easter Sunday was so akin to what Mom would do in a new body that I had to smile.

So, take this as you wish. For me, it was beautiful and magical. She earned her freedom. We were lucky enough to spend time with our family of the heart,

Signs and Miracles

Dennis, Jen, and Logan for the holiday. It was different. I'm still grateful for those we had at our proverbial table. Time is so precious.

Four days later, the second of the swallowtails emerged. She and the two others had been laid as eggs on the carrots Mom had planted in the raised garden bed. Three had stayed and made cocoons there too. I saved them by tying their carrot stalks that would wilt during winter and put them in the butterfly tent. Their miraculous tiny bodies did the rest.

Swallowtails even make a type of antifreeze so they can winter over and emerge safely in the spring. This is what the beloved monarchs cannot do, unfortunately. The monarch butterfly cannot live through the cold winter where it freezes. They therefore have to fly to the Mexican border in order to stay warm enough to survive. In my view, both the regal monarch and the black swallowtail are miraculous. One flies thousands of miles over generations to survive. The other makes antifreeze and uses mimicry to resemble the branch where it makes a cocoon. They both hibernate and then emerge in the Springtime. We are more alike than we are different, even with the differences of each of the species. They achieve their same end goals.

The second swallowtail was in stark contrast to the first. She was patient and let us all hold her. I got several photos of her on my camera and my phone. She flew off once to the neighbor's azalea and let me bring her back again so that my daughter could get to hold her too. The portraits of the second butterfly were beautiful. What a gift it was!

In October of 2019, on her own birthday, my mom sent a card to an address that didn't exist. She didn't realize that at the time, of course. While organizing papers on the porch from the last three or four decades of her life; she came across a special greeting card and knew that it needed to go to two of the dearest people in her life. She carefully wrote the beloved words she needed to say and then put the stamp on and put it in the mailbox.

A few days later, she panicked and said "I think I sent it to the wrong address. What do I do?" I said that it would show up when it was meant to get there. Somehow, I knew that would be true. Mom called and thanked them with her whole heart, not knowing what would become of that mismarked card. She still hoped the card would get to them, of course.

Months went by. In the beginning of February her dear friends got that card. She had passed away eight months prior. And there in the mail a week after they had to say goodbye to their beloved kitty they got to read Mom's thank you for their beautiful friendship. Mom loved animals more than words could express. She would be there to comfort her friends if she could. How fitting is it that the very late thank you card was there to comfort them when they most needed that very thing? What a miracle!

What does one talk about when they're actually present in the moment? Mom talked about how great the food tasted and gratitude for all the little acts of love people showed her. She expressed her love for people and animals and life in general. Mom also talked about miracles.

Most of her life, Mom did what I hear a lot of Libras do. She weighed the scales of each decision. She didn't often come down hard on one side or another in a discussion. When it came to miracles and 2020, she was firm. Her hazel eyes shone with determination that

Signs and Miracles

she'd earned with the wisdom of time. Out of the blue, she would say to me that "a miracle would come out of this."

"I'm certain of it," she would say. It was as if she was speaking about the sun rising the next day. She had never been so certain of anything in her whole life.

Words have power. Long had affirmations and positive thinking been a part of Mom's world. This was not in the same ballpark as that. It was if the lightning had struck her heart with the absolute knowledge that it was so. She just knew.

As time went by, she altered the statement a bit. "Someone will get a miracle out of this situation. I just don't know if it's me or someone else." The knowing didn't change in her eyes even as she realized the cancer had spread. Even in her last moments, she did not alter that statement.

You could argue that her miracle was completing the work of her life. Some people say no to that work their entire lives. She rose to the considerable challenges and met them with faith and love. She did the business of her life. She loved her children as best she knew how. She shared her wisdom with them along the way. She desperately tried to make them feel they were loved. She wanted each of us to really soak in the love like sponges. She wanted us to be filled up to dripping with it. She knew that if we got that very important knowing, then we would be okay with anything life would throw at us.

It was a miracle that I survived COVID. My throat was swollen shut with huge, overworked tonsils. My lungs filled with fluid and ached with pneumonia-like symptoms. It took a month for me to clear the fluid. It took a year and a half to have a regular heartbeat and to be able to exercise again.

From the moment I felt my body giving up, I have climbed the stairs towards health. One day at a time, I did more than the day before. The fact that I'm healthy again is nothing short of a miracle. Gratitude saturates each day I have on this earth. It seeps in through the day to day cracks. The whole of me at times was held afloat by gratitude for each day.

I am filled with gratitude that Mom did not die alone. That cancer would have been ravaging her body whether we knew about it or not. Whether she had moved here or not she would've been taken from this earth when it was her time. I'm grateful because of time. I got one more Thanksgiving, one more Christmas, one more birthday with her and so did my children. In fact, because we have lived in separate states for twenty plus years I got to catch up on twenty years with her. We talked on the phone almost daily before that point. We did a lot of healing in our relationship. Being on the phone isn't quite the same as being in person. When I told my fantastic instructor what had kept me away from dance class for so long, she, like everyone else said she was sorry. Once again, I got to tell the gratitude story. The story of extra time is what I carry with me.

I miss her. Of course I miss her. The ultimate miracle is that she and I really did do the work that we had set between us. I made what would be her very last coffee on this earth. If you knew my mother, you knew how much she loved her coffee. For me to be able to stand there just stirring her coffee in her hospital room as she laid there not able to get out of bed but coming alive with excitement in her eyes; it was a miracle.

Signs and Miracles

Miracles come in all shapes and sizes. For Mom and I, the miracle of a lifetime together ended up being shaped like coffee.

I remember my dad at the dinner table each night praying for patience, tolerance, and gratitude. That attitude was generated within him. It burns within all of us like an eternal flame. All we have to do is feed the right fire. Signs and tiny things I call miracles feed me in the emotionally challenging times. They anchor me. They also give rise to more thought, more love, and more joy.

Miracles come in all shapes and sizes. For Mom and I, the miracle of a lifetime together ended up being shaped like coffee.

Soul Fire

Angels

Things happen for a reason around me. Whatever you name it, I've seen it time and time again. I trust in that. Sometimes angels come to soften the blows of grief.

Soul Fire

Some people say that angels are around to help us when we need it. Some people think that their loved ones who have passed on send them signs. Some say that God sends us angels to protect us. Others think that the living can be angels in their lives. I've had my own share of angels in my life. One angel in particular arrived four years late and right on time.

My Aunt Sue has always loved angels. When we first started to get close, I was a young adult. That year, she cross stitched me a small, almost wallet sized angel. She sent it in a gold picture frame that year for Christmas. She was my angel in so many ways for years. She'd sold me a car for one dollar when my car died. I was still in college and had already fixed the engine once. A second time wasn't going to happen while I was trying to finish my bachelor's degrees. "We have to go to the courthouse and fill out papers. In order for it to be a sale, money has to change hands of at least one dollar. So, Uncle Ray and I would like to sell you the LeSabre for one dollar." I gratefully reached into my purse and handed them one dollar at the courthouse and we signed. The metallic green Buick was now my car. It turned out, like so many things in my life, to be a blessing in disguise. A few short months later I would hurt my back while working as an EMT. A disk in my neck was out of place for six months.

If you've never ridden in a Buick, they are remarkably smooth vehicles. The suspension is like butter. When I first got hurt, I tried riding in other cars. One friend had a truck. Another had a four-wheel drive with extra-large mud tires. In each case when someone drove over a bump, it was like an electric eel had set off the electric chair in my neck and spine. The pain took my breath away. It was a bit better if someone drove

Angels

my Buick. It was the least painful when I drove the Buick myself, however. When I handed my aunt that single dollar, I had no clue that for a while, that would be the only car I could ride in. Without that car, I wouldn't have been able to get anywhere during that time without a lot of tears and pain. My aunt and uncle were my angels.

Have you ever had a strange coincidence that helped ease your mind immeasurably? I have had that happen more times than I can count. It could be that our technical brains just add story to things that have no inherent meaning. Sometimes there are so many coincidences that happen that one must document them. I have grown past trying to explain things away, or justify, or rationalize. When I die someday, I will gain insight I don't have here on Earth. And, for now, I'm grateful for the angels.

Mom and I went to a new age store when she moved closer to us in 2019. It was one of her happy places. She'd spent hours reading their books. This time though, we both knew that she went for another purpose: crystals. She'd always loved crystals of all sorts. They made her happy and she really enjoyed studying their different metaphysical properties. That's not for everyone, but it was a passion of hers. We walked over to the counter and she slowly and carefully looked at each one. Some were in cases and others were in baskets. At last, she'd found the one she wanted in a basket near the checkout counter of the gift store. "Ah ha," Mom said with the childlike gleam in her eyes.

"Is this the one you want?" I asked her.

"This one's perfect," she said. She turned her hand over and uncurled her fingers. There in the soft palm of her left hand was a unakite pink and mossy green angel. She was about an inch tall, slender, and made of stone.

Before long, Mom would be diagnosed with cancer, and in less than a year she would be gone from this earth. When she died, I found that little angel in her purse. She had carried her with her every single day. As with many things of Moms, I knew that when the time was right to pass that on, I would know.

Jen's text came in at 9:45 PM one night. Her stepmom had passed though her battle with metastatic cancer had been a valiant one. She would answer you honestly if you asked her how she was doing. She didn't complain too much though. She fought cancer with grace and dignity and her head held high. Just days afterwards, Jen's husband Dennis completed his own treatment for cancer on Veteran's Day. The Navy veteran completed radiation on Veteran's Day. You couldn't have planned that if you tried.

Jen's stepmom had been in Jen's life for over thirty years at that point. Naturally, I had to go to the funeral with her. We were all vaccinated. After all my children had endured in the last years, it didn't make sense to bring the whole family to the funeral. When I packed for the trip, I found my Mom's angel with my lipstick. She was waiting. This was the time. Quietly, I slipped her into my pocket, told my family I loved them, and left.

Jen had held dinner for me until I got there. It was a delicious spaghetti with salad. After dinner and shared stories, her eyes lit up and she said, "I have something for you." Never in a million years would I have guessed what she would hand me. The small thin item was wrapped in that grayish paper that most stores wrap

Angels

your glass items in. I knew it must be somewhat fragile. I thought maybe there was some craft her stepmom had made and she thought I should have it. But really, I couldn't imagine what it was.

Slowly, I opened the paper and laying there was a beautiful hand painted porcelain angel. "Oh, it's beautiful," I exclaimed, forgetting about the one in my pocket. I honestly didn't recognize it. I turned it over wondering who had made it and was taken aback. My name and "2017" were printed there in my handwriting. Suddenly, I remembered. Jen had packed us and the three children up one day and taken us to the paint your own pottery place. My father and my husband were both in the hospital with aneurysms and a stroke at the same time that year. Dad was in the hospital with aneurysm replacement surgery and on a ventilator. He would pass away a short time after we visited the pottery place. Was it days later? A week? I don't remember. I had again forced myself to live and to create memories and something outside of people being sick.

My son painted a small bat with purple, black, and speedy gusto to get the job done as soon as humanly possible. My daughter on the other hand chose pretty paints and took her time slathering the paint onto her mermaid plate. My niece worked thoughtfully. I took ages to find the right thing to paint. My chest was tight with worry and fresh tears filled my eyes. Then I saw her. There was a beautiful, three and a half inch, flat angel ornament. She had a halo, and grooves to create a full color palate on her dress. With the drip of every color of the rainbow, I prayed to God that she would signify healing for my dad.

Soul Fire

A month went by I think before we picked up our pottery. Jen offered to go get it because she knew how hard I'd taken Dad's death. When I saw her though, a month after that there was only the two that my children had painted. "I can't find yours. These two were alone. I'm so sorry," she said.

"It's ok," I said. "It's probably for the best. Maybe someone else needed it more. Or maybe it got damaged in the kiln." I barely had the energy to breathe and put my clothes on each day. I wasn't worried about the angel at that juncture. So, imagine my surprise looking down at that very angel for the first time again. Her glazes that were once pastel were vibrant reds, purples, yellows, and blues. I figured when I never saw it again that it was not the right promise. My dad was healed, but not at all in the way I had prayed for back then.

Once the shock wore off that I had painted the angel, it dawned on me. "You're never going to guess what I have in my pocket," I said. I slowly pulled out the small unakite angel. "I brought this for you, Dennis." It brought Mom a lot of strength when she was going through her cancer. May it bring you strength as well." I took a photo of the porcelain angel and slid it back across the table "I think she's meant to be with you all," I said. I sat back in awe and wonder.

Things happen for a reason around me. Whatever you name it, I've seen it time and time again. I trust in that. When I saw the look on Dennis and Jen's faces, I knew that the angels had found their true homes. They weren't late. They weren't even four years late. They were right on time. Once again, I found myself filled with gratitude and wonder. The Universe is so very big. We are never ever alone. That old adage, "Be still and listen," is sometimes all it takes to find the right path.

Angels

Losing someone is never easy. Saying goodbye to someone you love leaves a hole in your heart. Grief is love forever changed by death. Love always remains though. Sometimes angels come to soften the blows of that grief. Sometimes they say "Hi. I still exist." The hope and prayer is that with time, the love is bigger than the pain. Love is what I believe we are meant to feel on this planet. Every single day is filled with a million tiny moments. May we use those moments to their fullest with love.

The hope and prayer is that with time, the love is bigger than the pain.

Soul Fire

WWDD: What Would Dad Do?

 *When those we love are gone from this earth, we still wish we could ask their advice.*

What would Dad tell me to do? What words of wisdom would he have had when times were hard? What would he tell me to do now? That's a fantastic question. When those we love are gone from this earth, we still wish we could ask their advice. Dad never pulled any punches or held much back. He didn't hold back even when it hurt to hear. Usually though, he was kind, loving, and tender where my heart was concerned.

If Dad were alive, he would stir slowly from his slumber. He would've stayed up late into the wee hours of the night just because he could. Mornings would begin around 10:00 AM. He would roll the beautiful warm green blanket back and sit up. Then he'd affirm: "This is going to be a GOOD Day!" His hands would be open on his thighs, palms facing up as he uttered those words. He would open the blinds to his room. If my daughter was there, he would ask her, "Would you like to ride with Ride Guy and open the blinds to a brand-new day?" The smile on his face would be so genuine. She'd say yes with a huge smile and climb onto his lap in the wheelchair. He'd tell her to hold on as he wheeled towards his two windows. From her perch on his lap, she'd be just tall enough to reach the rod on the blinds to open them. He would let her do it and secretly help her turn the blinds. The bright white sunlight would pour in through the wooden painted blinds. She'd slide off his lap and go off to play. He'd make his oatmeal and sit at the table. We would meet there at the table, looking out on the Monet garden and chat.

"How do you think I'm doing Dad?" I would ask him with a hopeful air to my voice. I would hope he would be proud of me. He'd take a big bite of his thick

WWDD: What Would Dad Do?

oatmeal with the large tablespoon and think. He'd look at the garden, pondering. Then, he would speak.

"You're doing a lot of growing right now. You are doing the work of your life sharing your story. Much like the tomato babies under the grow lights, you are cultivating your crops for the world. You're working hard, Sweet Baby." He would call me this even at forty some years old. I wouldn't mind because it was Dad. He could get away with things that no one else would dare try. The birds would chirp in the trees in the yard. He would close his eyes and smile, listening to the sweet songs.

"Change is coming," Dad would say. He'd have some astrological reasoning for the precise challenges at hand. "You can handle it though. You will barely recognize yourself when this year is over. Let the wave take you where it will. Don't give up even when it's scary. Especially when it's scary, dig in deeper and dig your way out. The hole isn't going to be as big as you think it is while you're in the thick of it." Sage advice would come pouring out with love and thoughtfulness. He would glance outside again. "How's the yard? Will you get out there today? I see the hyacinths and daffodils are blooming. The rose bushes are leafing out. I love how Spring comes sooner down here."

"I weeded that bed next to the neighbors yesterday. Nothing happened. A year ago, I couldn't breathe, just bending over to pick up one weed. Yesterday, nothing happened at all out of the ordinary. The nasty sticky weed that gives you a rash was removed though. John took down the dilapidated white picket fence. While it was down, I figured I'd weed the beds." Shock would be behind my voice. Dad would hear that with his keen ears.

"You've come through the "Eye of the Storm." He carried you through, like my song. You get to breathe now." A smile would cross his thin lips and he would really take in how sweet it was to simply weed the garden. He'd look down at his clean hands and short fingernails. He'd chew a cuticle or two. "It felt good to get your hands in the dirt, didn't it?" He would ask. I'd smile, feeling really known and shake my head yes.

Dad would tell me to take it easy on my husband, "Let him rest too. Don't forget to rest yourselves. It all goes by so quickly. There will always be more to do." He would listen to how I'd done dance class for the first time in a year. He'd ask how it went. "You really are healing, Sarah. You're emerging from this a different person than you went in. Really take in how this has molded you like the clay. Your shackles are gone now. The sky's the limit. You've had to take it slower than you would have liked. That's all okay." He wouldn't mean to be contradicting himself. He would be perfectly honest with all he said. Life was too short for small talk that was meaningless. Dad was full of the good stuff.

The weather had warmed up with the daylight savings time weekend. "Do you want to go out on the porch Dad? It's nice out. We could listen to the birds better there."

"Sure, let's go. Let me take care of my bowl," Dad would say as he finished the oatmeal and let the silver tablespoon clank in the white porcelain bowl.

"I'll take it Dad," I would say as I reached out and took it from him. I'd fill the bowl with warm water in the right side of the double sink. The sunlight would fall on my face like a warm sheer curtain. I'd close my eyes in bliss for a moment, taking it in. *There's more outside,* I'd think. I'd turn away from the sink and head

WWDD: What Would Dad Do?

for the back door and hold it open for him.

Dad would barely get out of the door with his walker as the dog ran by him. He would wait, wagging his tail to see where Dad would sit. Once he sat down, Buster would jump up on the couch and put his head on Dad's left thigh. An onlooker would think that the big dog would've knocked him over. If you really looked though, you'd see that the dog waited and gave Dad just enough clearance to walk and move. His whole fawn colored body moved side to side with the wagging of his tail. The excitement was palpable. And he waited.

So many times, these past two years, I've felt like Buster. I was in a body that was ailing and slower than I wanted it to be. I was chomping at the bit like a horse ready to canter and gallop. Yet, I was forced to be patient and wait. "You've done your waiting," Dad would say.

The conversation would meander like the curving beds in the back yard. He would listen to all the ways I'd trimmed the rosebushes and how I thought they'd be great this year. "They're finally evening out in height to each other. The purple and white true roses are catching up to the yellow knockout bush."

Again, I'd think that he was the only reason the yellow one was still there. He got so much enjoyment out of yellow roses in particular. *Look how it dwarfs the others,* I'd think to myself.

"What was it like for you back then?" Dad would ask. "What was it like to not be able to weed the yard or dance when you wanted to?" His eyes would be thoughtful and he would give me all of his attention.

"I was impatient. I knew even then that it would not last. And yet, sometimes, I wondered. I wondered if it would be exactly that way forever. The answer always came in the quiet though. This was temporary. I knew that."

Dad would nod his head yes. The light and slight breeze would catch his curly silver hair. He'd ask me when his haircut was scheduled for. "My Bill Clinton haircut is getting a bit long. I think I need the short Bill Clinton."

This statement always struck me as odd. Occasionally, Dad would cross the aisle so to speak. He never spoke ill of Bill. We all knew that 'Bush Jr.' was his favorite though. He was so proud that his stroke recovery book was in George W. Bush's presidential library. He even framed the card that the administration had sent him that year.

"You're going to be okay," Dad would say after a pause. "You've made it through the worst of it. I know it felt like forever. In an odd way, you understand what it's like to be a gimp like me now. You have more empathy for people like your mother too with her COPD. Isn't it odd how life works?"

Yes. Yes, it is. Countless days and nights I've wished that I could talk with Dad like we used to when he was here. The truth is that if I'm still and listen, I could in fact tell you exactly what Dad would say. He would encourage me where I'd worked hard. He would call me on my crap if I wasn't being fair. He'd wax philosophical and spiritual. He would always, always live vicariously through my garden experiences. He missed gardening once he couldn't physically do it anymore. He knew the beauty of helping things grow. He knew the magic of the bulbs and seeds popping out of the dark brown earth. He reveled in it right alongside of me.

If time and space and death didn't separate us, Dad

WWDD: What Would Dad Do?

would say that every passing is unique. "We each have our own journey to take on this plane and the next." He'd look up at the sky and the thin wispy clouds as if he saw someone up there painting in the sky. "Until we walk the path, we don't know where the journey will lead." Then, he'd listen to the cardinal's chirp and the squirrels chase each other in the yard.

Dad was a natural writer and poet. His quick wit was something magnificent to behold. One Christmas after his first stroke, I called him to wish him a Merry Christmas. "I love you, Dad. You're a magnificent creature and I'm so proud of all the work you've done." I left it on his answering machine. He picked up before I hung up and laughed.

"Did Zafi put you up to that phrase?" he asked. I could tell he was smiling and sighed with relief.

"No Dad. That one was all me." I assured him. That particular phrase sounded good enough to be one of his. He was an impeccable wordsmith.

The very best of my father came out around me. He told me that often. He called me the snake charmer in one of the pieces he wrote. He referred to himself as the snake, cold blooded with scales. He had the sage advice, words of wisdom, and just the right amount of listening when he was at his best.

He told me I could be anything in the whole wide world. He told me I could be anyone I wanted to be. As an adult, we sat and talked for hours upon hours about anything and everything. He was my sounding board while John was at sea. He was my gardener of the heart. Usually, I brought the dirt, pots and tomato seeds to the kitchen table so he could plant them. One year he even used his walker to get to the raised garden beds and planted the tomato babies with me. He really got me all the way to my core.

Some people understand you all the way to your core, the heart and soul of you. Dad was like that for me. He understood who I was, who I wanted to be, and what mattered to me. On the topic of education, he always said to get the degree. "I don't care if you get it in underwater basket weaving but get that bachelor's degree girl. Education is the key to success and getting a good job." He said it with such conviction that I simply knew it was truth. Sometimes, when he'd tell me a particularly juicy bit of his past, he'd say "I'm sorry if I tell you too much. I don't want you to be in the dark like I was." I never felt that his sharing was anything to be sorry for though. His humanity laid bare and naked. He shared of his soul that way. It rang true in my soul then.

WWDD? What Would Dad Do? What would Dad say right now if he could? He would tell me to write. "Get it done, girl. Someone needs to hear what you have to say. You'll never know until it's done what the impact will be. Just do it." He'd be a veritable cornucopia of metaphors. They would roll off his tongue like honey falling off a saturated piece of toast. Ultimately, Dad would tell me to follow my dreams. "Plant the seeds for the fruit you want in your life. Water them. Love them. Raise them knowing they're loved. Be patient with them. Be more patient with them than I was with you. Be more like your mother where patience is concerned. Don't forget boundaries. They save your butt when your heart gets you into trouble."

Dad would wax philosophical then and ponder which is more important, the head or the heart. He would settle in his heart regardless of the pain. He would tell me to follow each and everything my gut tells

WWDD: What Would Dad Do?

me to do in this life. "Life is too short and too sweet to waste it," he would say. Of this, he would be absolutely certain.

Whether you have someone in your life like Dad or not, you do now. He would be your surrogate Dad if you needed one. He was exactly that to many people. You have me in your corner, cheering you on. I may not know you or your particular struggles. I may not know your exact set of life skills or obstacles along the way. I do know that you are a magnificent creature.

You deserve to follow your dreams. You deserve to believe in the beauty of the world and that there is more good out there than bad. You deserve love. We all do. If you need a cheerleader, I will volunteer. Life is too short and too sweet. If something keeps nagging at your soul, then follow it. If your gut instinct a.k.a. intuition tells you something, listen. Listen to that still small voice. You may call it anything that makes sense to you. That inner knowing will not steer you wrong. It will save you from many things if you let it. It will give you your Soul Fire back if you've lost it, or even your smile.

Hopefully there is someone in your life cheering for your wellbeing and following your dreams. Sometimes they speak quietly to not be too judgmental. The whisper on the breeze may be the answer to your query. Above all, Dad would say follow your gut, your guides. Don't be afraid of failure. Within the failures, there are lessons for success.

If Dad were here today and we could do anything at all, we'd go walk in a garden. He'd have his Martin guitar slung over his shoulder and we'd walk holding hands. He'd have his jeans on and an emerald green V-neck shirt. His feet would be donned with the brown leather deck shoes without socks. The confinement of socks simply would not do for him.

We would walk without a goal in mind or a destination. Each path of the garden would meander to the next and the next. We would ponder the plants, insects, birds, and squirrels along the way. Dad would stop, gently grab my shoulders and look me square in the eyes. He would say, "Sweet baby, you can be anything you want to be in this lifetime. All you have to do is choose and go for it." He would laugh and hug me and hold me tight and tell me he loved me. He would say time and death do not erase love. "There is never enough time with those we love," Dad always said. "You already know what to do. Deep down, you know."

My mom would have always argued with that. "Sometimes, people don't know," she would say. Leave space for not knowing.

Take the road less traveled. Dare to be a dreamer. More than that, dare to make your dreams a reality. It's always worth it. Always.

Life is too short and too sweet. Listen to that still small voice. It will give you your Soul Fire back if you've lost it, or even your smile.

The Painted Desert Life

If we listen to the inspiration, the call, the gut instinct, then we hear the heartbeat of the Universe.

Having grown up on the east coast, I barely knew what the desert looked like, let alone the Painted Desert. I always wanted to travel growing up. Being a military spouse, I got my chance. One such time, my husband and I were moving from the west coast back east. We had two cars, a cat, and a house full of furniture to get across country. No big deal.

This move, I went east first with one car and the cat. I had to get the next house together while my husband finished out that duty station. Driving three thousand plus miles alone would be rather boring. The cat didn't like to travel and didn't talk much.

Once again, Dennis came to my rescue. Dennis was Jen's husband and more like a brother to me than a friend. For an independent personality, I sure did get rescued a lot, I noted. My husband John and I picked him up from the airport. Time was short and we were about to get in the car and travel.

"What would you like to do?" I asked him.

"Let's go see a sunset in California. They're the best. I haven't seen one in a long time." He breathed in deeply and turned his face to the bright Southern California sun. A smile crossed his bearded face as he took in the moment.

How long had it been since Dennis had a vacation, I wondered. Ages, I suspected. He went right from the Navy to a different job as an IT professional for an expanding tanning company. His job as their computer guru was never ending. He was on call for the boss and all the employees any time day or night. He was a one man show and squeezed in vacations in between calls. Even dinners often were flanked with calls. He didn't mind really. He liked being useful. He really liked being

The Painted Desert Life

appreciated for what he did. His years in the Navy left him not knowing how to take a break though.

San Diego was a gorgeous city. I had wasted my time there really. I didn't explore enough, or see enough while I was free to do so. Yet, here we were heading east. That sun was setting in more than one way. We were leaving good friends behind there. John had to work on the ship as I got the house ready back east. So, Dennis came out to drive with me across the country.

The very next morning, we had loaded the car and charged the cameras. We were taking the southern route. I felt like an outlaw, stealing a vacation with my dear friend. A pang of guilt and sadness came that our spouses couldn't join us on the trip. I told myself that we would do this all together one day.

The Joshua trees gave rise to the desert and the cacti along the highway. He'd grown up in Arizona and grew more at ease with every mile. The worries of the world dropped away as we drove, despite him being tired from his yearly bout of bronchitis. He slept a lot as I drove. That didn't matter to me though. He needed the rest to heal.

Knowing this was a once in a lifetime type thing, Dennis was determined to show me Phoenix and the Painted Desert. We planned it all out so we would get to the Painted Desert area just before sunset, in the golden hour. The stars were aligned perfectly, it seemed. He told me how beautiful it was there near the Four Corners and the Grand Canyon area. We didn't have time to see the Grand Canyon. The Petrified Forest National Park sits just off Route 40 though. There's a small loop drive that doesn't really take you too far off the highway. It was perfect.

Soul Fire

No one was behind us as we drove into the park. The red, orange, and tan rocky hills were breathtaking. I ran into the gift shop and grabbed some petrified wood for Mom. She loved crystals and rocks and the Southwest. Five minutes in the store and back on the road.

The petrified tree logs were huge. We stopped the car and took silly photos of ourselves trying to pick them up. The car slowed to a stop on the crest of a small hill where the red hills got closer. He pulled the car to the side of the road and opened the sunroof. I took off my shoes and stood on the passenger seat, holding my camera.

The cat looked at me from his hiding place next to my black flip flops. He was not fond of the car. His mostly black fur blended into the floor like a tiny fur rug. His eyes were huge as he stared up at me. He looked like a wild animal, so scared by all the movement. We had to get him across country somehow, though. The car was better than being cargo in an airplane. "It's ok, Trouble," I told him as I petted him with my bare foot.

The dry wind was warm but cooling off as the sun went down. I kept shooting as fast as my fingers allowed. Dennis had his camera and shot photos from the driver's seat. Sometimes I took his and took a few from my perch. My white t-shirt rippled in the wind. I felt like a bird flying. This was God's country. Every second the light changed as the blue of the sky turned to yellow, and then gave way to purples and deep blues. I sat down and we continued slowly on the trek towards the exit. Five miles an hour felt fast, like we were frozen in time. The road curved over a small hill and to the left just as the sun kissed the horizon line to

The Painted Desert Life

our left. With shock I said, "Look over there! It's an old car!"

Sure enough, a rusted out old model T was sitting there waiting for us to take more photos. We filled our artistic hearts and cameras as fast as our fingers could push the buttons. We took turns posing in front of the car. The sunset behind us changed by the second and we had to be fast. It didn't matter. We made each second count.

Before long, the stars emerged in the royal blue sky. The park closed at dark and we had to go. We snapped our last photos and slowly rolled off into the night and back onto Route 40. That old car felt like the perfect nod to the old Route 66 we were paralleling. Progress gave way to Route 40 sometime after WW2. For just a moment, we had a time machine of wonder and awe. What a gift! I profusely thanked Dennis for suggesting such a thing, again feeling guilty that Jen and John couldn't join us. Jen was pregnant though and traveling wasn't really in the cards for her at present. John was otherwise disposed with the Navy.

I knew even then that it was an immensely powerful and special moment. I had no idea that it would make Dennis' top five memories though. Dad used to say that we were lucky if we could count on one hand the number of lifelong solid friendships in our lives. I've made some fantastic friends over the years. They've become family in turn a fair amount of the time. Gratitude and wonder were overflowing on that trip. This world was worth protecting. Once again that filled my soul as it had many times before. Seeing nature and the earth we have been blessed enough to live on reinforced that thought each and every time. The

Painted Desert and Petrified National Forest were an absolute highlight in my life.

Years later at dinner, Dennis regaled the tale of the Painted Desert with our family. He and Jen had one child and we had our two by then. That same gleam of joy filled his eyes as the memory flooded back. Was it the Southwest that held his heart? Was it the vacation in a life of working? I think it was being in the presence of the beauty in this world that stopped and held his heart so dearly. It moved him.

That which stirs the soul has value beyond words. If the heart is moved enough to take you out of the mundane everyday monotony, then heed the call. Allow the sights and sounds to fill every cell of your being. Let it flow through you and inspire you. I cannot help but believe that we are meant to be moved in such a way. It is most certainly unique for each of us. Standing in the presence of that beauty, we are connected to it deeply. When we drive out of our own Painted Deserts, and back to our lives, does it not fuel us? The memories pop up and carry us down the river towards our next big ideas. They meander from small to large like the great Colorado River. Sometimes it's so convoluted that we don't remember what started us down the river.

The journey is worth it. Through the twists and turns of life we are inspired. We are called to share our story, to be our own architects in this world. If we listen to the inspiration, the call, the gut instinct, then we hear the heartbeat of the Universe. It beats in time with all of us and yet is entirely its own entity. Is it God? Is it Mother Earth? Is it our collective unconscious? Maybe it's all of them together. Maybe we are all like the redwoods in California with roots deep in the ground. Maybe we're all connected somehow and feeding each other deep within the earth. Do the trees know they're connected? Do they feel it? Some say they do. You decide. I'd like to think they feel that connection.

We as humans have grown numb to the connection as of late. We search for it in mind numbing ways like social media. Deep down though, is it not that connection which feeds our souls like mothers' milk? I believe it is that oneness rather than aloneness that feeds us. Sometimes what feeds your soul is being alone and the quiet listening that can only come in that space. And eventually, even if it's a rare treat, we seek out the connection once again.

I pray that you have your own Painted Desert. I believe this is what Thoreau meant by sucking the marrow out of life. Dad used to literally suck the marrow from chicken wings. That totally grossed me out when I was younger. I never quite understood that. Maybe it's simply getting all the goodness out of something as in life. If you don't have those moments of freedom, beauty, and joy in your life, give yourself permission to go find them.

Soul Fire

 *That which stirs the soul has value beyond words. If the heart is moved enough to take you out of the mundane everyday monotony, then heed the call.*

Grace and Kindness

It took a village to get through really tough times. The life raft was built with many hands. The main ingredient was love. I learned that it wasn't a weakness to allow the love. It took strength to pass the baton, even for a moment.

We all need grace and kindness. There are times when we find ourselves in a situation that we would not have intentionally chosen for ourselves. Each of us around the globe has been through something profound and unique. Many of us lost those we love. Many of us had COVID. Each of us had a story regardless.

We all have the triumphs and tribulations that led us to today. We also have the tiny miracles if we look for them. We are more alike than we are different, no matter where we come from. Compassion does not have to equal agreement. One can choose to be kind to anyone without agreeing with everything they say. Our cultures are varied, beautiful, and unique. They are all worthy.

You are here for a reason. You deserve to fulfill on the quiet dreams you keep in the recesses of your soul. Give yourself permission to be brave. I promise that it's worth it.

COVID is the reason I started writing this story, but it's not really about COVID at all. Soul Fire is about human resilience, love, and overcoming. It's about believing in yourself and digging deep into your heart to find the strength to endure.

You're not alone. Each and every story is unique. If you find someone who can listen, you will see that empathy is strong within other humans. Even though some things have grown especially ugly in the past few years, humans, at their core, have not collectively completely given up hope. **There is still good in this world.** I promise you. I've seen it.

The grace and kindnesses may sometimes be whispers in the middle of a great storm. They are no less real. People still care about other people. They've just been through their own version of a war zone of sorts. They may not be combat veterans. But we've all been through a lot these past years. Healing takes time. It's going to require more than a billion ventilators to heal our souls. We can do it. We will do it.

In order to come back to my own health, I had to be kind to myself in ways I never dreamt I'd have to be. Naively, and perhaps even egotistically, I thought I'd never be in such a position. Yet, instinctively at the beginning of COVID I knew that I would get it. I knew that the online dance class could be the difference between life and death. As I walked with Mom's cancer journey, I knew the risks. I walked by her side, holding her hand with grace, kindness, and love. That was what there was to do.

Now, we all have to heal. Step by step, dream by dream, we are all rebuilding a future for ourselves. We all thought that we'd live a certain life and have certain things happen. I doubt many of us predicted the past several years. Yet, here we are.

Two years to the day from the shutdown I took another online dance class class. Do you know? I didn't pass out. I didn't almost faint a dozen times. I even weeded the yard that week. I simply was able to put the sticky weeds into the bag and move on. It was just dance class. It was just weeding the yard. I noted with wonder that there was no fallout from dance class like there had been since I got sick. The stark contrast felt like silence after a bomb had exploded. When I picked up the sticky weeds, there were no black spots in my peripheral vision. I did not get short of breath. Who knew that I would be so very happy to weed the yard? It was brilliant.

Soul Fire

Accepting help from anyone was not easy for me. Fierce independence and help didn't go together well in the same sentence. The fact was undeniable that those who loved me held my heart with such care that they fed my Soul Fire. They sat quietly in the forest tending the fire in the middle of the night, surrounded by the darkness. They held the faith that I didn't have in that moment. They knew the sun would rise again. They knew the storms would pass. They loved me through the darkness and helped me love myself.

As a teenager, I was in danger. I was also loved beyond measure, beyond what I believed I deserved. During the Aneurysm Alley years, those who loved me saw me completely empty. They carefully tended my fire with such kindness. Jen was there every step of the way. Neighbors and loved ones helped in small and large ways when I needed it. My cousin drove halfway across the country to pray with my father the night before his surgery. My childhood friend came to be with us when my husband had brain surgery. The independence in me protested each time. Yet, I was so empty. Each kindness filled me with such enormous gratitude. It was in those moments that I understood the deepest meaning of the word: Gratitude.

I didn't have the strength to fight the help in those moments. Instead, I said thank you. They saw the hot tears in my eyes and how much I felt the love. The trips to the pottery place or some random store, the walks, and each act of kindness were felt in repeated waves. They covered my open raw wounds with love, care, and concern. It took a village to get through really tough times. The life raft was built with many hands. The main ingredient was love.

Grace and Kindness

Often, I was my own biggest obstacle. People who cared wanted to help. I didn't know how to let them. It took every experience in my life to come to a head in order to learn how to accept contribution from others. Grace and kindness were out there with outstretched arms my whole life. I couldn't believe that I deserved them. Therefore, I could not see them. When words failed, people came with a hug or a random get together. They got through the cracks in my shattered armor. Time and my own willingness let that broken armor fall away. I learned that it wasn't a weakness to allow the love. It took strength to pass the baton, even for a moment.

I do not know where I would be without those who loved me along the way. A small thing, such as a smile of a stranger, meant the world to me, especially when I was emotionally empty. Friends and family couldn't fix the difficult circumstances I faced. There have been many things in my life I couldn't fix. I couldn't change the events of my teen years. I couldn't fix my parents death. I couldn't undo that fabric tearing of our lives. I couldn't change the fact that my husband had six strokes and a brain aneurysm. There are some things that are unfixable.

I could focus on what was possible. I could allow the mocha goodness to fill up my senses with love. I could buy milkweed for the monarchs after Dad died. I could tent the black swallowtails that wintered over on the carrots Mom had planted. I could create art, photographing each butterfly that emerged newly. When one wintered over underneath my back porch, I scooped up his one wing from between the wooden floorboards. I gently preserved him onto watercolor paper. I painted his caterpillar form munching on green milkweed leaves. I painted the sky behind him with sunshine and storm clouds alike. The grass was lush and vibrant green. The sky was blue. I mourned the loss of that life. I braided the fabric of my life together from the events of my past. I set him free on the page, flying off into the sun.

One by one, those brilliant butterflies come to my yard year after year. They waft in on the gentle summer breeze. They land on my lantana, butterfly weed, or my daylilies. They stir up creativity. We share moments together in the garden. Every monarch that crosses my path fuels my Soul Fire.

Every butterfly I give safe haven to is a life saved. Every flower, annual, perennial, native plant, or otherwise in my garden is one piece of the life I deliberately cultivate. I grow their food. I give the swallowtails and the monarchs places to safely make cocoons. I give them grace and kindness. This naturalist view gives me a literal embodiment of new life and personal growth. I see my parents on the wind and their wings. I see that love others have poured into me as I pass it on to these creatures. When I see someone else in pain, I create a space for them to breathe, process, and hopefully, to heal.

When the cloth of the past is tightly wrapped around, hiding me inside, it feels safe, for a time. Inevitably, the confines of that tiny space I've nestled myself in, high in a tree begins to feel confined, old, and no longer comfortable. I allow the change to happen. Learn what there is to learn. Give yourself that same permission to fly.

Sometimes, the old fear comes back. It passes. I think it will likely be with me forever in some form. Healing is a continuum that we revisit multiple times

Grace and Kindness

rather than something we do once. When it comes, I realize that it is a part of me. When my survivor shows up to protect me, I listen. I do not shove her out in the cold alone like I did in the past. I also realize that I get to say where I ultimately land and where I put my faith.

Grace and kindness were both required for me to step out of the shadows of my past. My change was motivated by purpose. It was worthwhile to change for me because I created the worth. I honored my values by growing up the little parts of myself. I honored myself every time I made space for all of me. Every bit of my old garbage that I took out is less that my children need to wade through. Cleaning house took time and tenderness.

My whole heart is not filled to the brim with fear any longer. The fear seeps in and oozes, especially when there is a storm. Recognizing that it's not here to stay is my biggest asset and inner strength now. I didn't have that as a child. I remember to stand taller when I remember who I am. I'm a survivor, full of vibrant pure Soul Fire. I'm more than my past, my pain, and my lessons. I'm here to stay. I'm here to live.

I cannot rush change, the perfect outcome, or my growth. The butterfly must spend a certain amount of time in the cocoon. It takes the time to reconfigure, alter, and change the body. When the process is complete, they must then fight their way out of that once beloved safe haven. It no longer serves them. They don't need it anymore. When the sun kisses their body, their wings are tiny and unable to fly for a time. Vulnerably, they must perch, wait, and move their energy in their life force from their once heavily used caterpillar body to their newly emerged wings. Purposefully, the wings bloom like flowers. They dry and ready themselves for flight with the warmth of the sun. Rushing will not make it so, no matter how much a butterfly may wish it could fly one moment sooner. I am that butterfly. You are that butterfly. Live.

I remember to stand taller when I remember who I am. I'm a survivor, full of vibrant pure Soul Fire. I'm more than my past, my pain, and my lessons. I'm here to stay. I'm here to live.

To all those who protected me along the way: Thank you. To the village that helped me create and repair the life raft: Thank you. Every kindness you showed me was meaningful and powerful.

We run this race ourselves. I acknowledge each of you as you navigate this marathon we call life. It takes something to keep fighting sometimes. Thank you for continuing to try, especially when it's hard. Thank you for letting in the lessons life offers you. You are your biggest asset. Allow yourself to believe. Thank you for going on this self-discovery journey with me. I am not the same person I was before I wrote this. I wrote it for you. Thank you for having faith in the whole kit and kaboodle.

I'm so grateful for every one of my friends and family, my village. I process out loud. It can be a lot to bear witness to and I'm grateful that they had the space in their hearts to listen. They eased the gut wrenching, soul sucking grief of losing my daddy. They walked beside me as disciples of faith during COVID. We had faith that it would end together. They gave me peace and filled my ever-draining bucket when my mom was dying. Many of you have been well-quoted throughout. Thank you for allowing your quotes to enrich this book immeasurably and for sharing your stories and lives with me. Thank you for my initial readers and ponderers who helped me so fervently work through what needed to be said. Thank you for your encouragement, love, and valuable insights.

Thank you to my past teacher, Ms. T who encouraged me to remember what got me through the hard times. You told me to show people what sustained me. That became the format for this book. Thank you

Acknowledgements

for walking beside me as my family. Your love gave me so much left unspoken. I'm eternally grateful.

My soul sisters, my ride or die few on the sojourn reminded me who I was repeatedly. You took me to paint pottery, to get pedicures, to watercolor retreats, to writing intensives. You sat with me as I cried at my parents' graveside, marveling at still being alive myself. You taught me about fluffy eggs and how to be secure inside of my own skin. You held me when I was in tatters. You held my babies. We held each other as we grew and lived. Thank you.

To my mentor, creative partner and developmental editor, Willa Mitchell, thank you for believing in the dream of this book. Thank you for guiding my learning. You always say, "You can't write through what you can't learn through." The process has been a beautiful, exquisite push and pull of growth and reflective pause. I will forever treasure this process you undertook willingly with me. I'm so grateful for your insights, skill set, and your wide-open heart and friendship. Most of all, thank you for encouraging me and holding me as I found my own voice. You didn't try to change me. Rather, you accepted, respected, and loved all of me.

Thank you to my editor Lindsey. You made me ask the hard questions.

And, to my husband, thank you for stepping into the spotlight. I know you'd much prefer the comfort of your library than being in a non-fiction book. Thank you for being not only an intimate part of this book, but also of the editing and publication process. You were my chief editor, formatter, researcher, and partner. Thank you for patiently loving me through all the light and the darkness. Thank you for encouraging and dreaming with me every step of the way. You helped me get the story out.

Soul Fire

www.ingramcontent.com/pod-product-compliance
Lightning Source LLC
Chambersburg PA
CBHW050257010526
44107CB00033B/1412/J